HISTORIC
COSTUMES
and
HOW TO
MAKE THEM

BANQUET IN LONDON, *temp*. EDWARD IV
British Museum MS. Royal E.4
Note the bag sleeve worn knotted at back

HISTORIC COSTUMES
and
HOW TO MAKE THEM

Mary Fernald and E. Shenton

DOVER PUBLICATIONS, INC.
Mineola, New York

Bibliographical Note

This Dover edition, first published in 2006, is an unabridged
republication of the work originally published as *Costume Design
and Making: A Practical Handbook* by Adam and Charles Black,
London, 1937.

Library of Congress Cataloging-in-Publication Data

Fernald, Mary.
   [Costume design & making]
   Historic costumes and how to make them : a practical hand-
book / by Mary Fernald in collaboration with Eileen Shenton.
      p. cm.
   Reprint. Originally published: London : Adam and Charles
Black, 1937. Under the title: Costume design & making.
   ISBN-13: 978-0-486-44906-7 (pbk.)
   ISBN-10: 0-486-44906-8 (pbk.)
   1. Costume design. 2. Costume—History. 3. Garment cutting.
I. Title.

PN2067.F4 2006
792.02'6—dc22

2006040239

Manufactured in the United States by LSC Communications
44906810   2019
www.doverpublications.com

CONTENTS

PAGE

INTRODUCTION 9

I. SAXON TO NORMAN 20

II. NORMAN TO PLANTAGENET 26

III. EDWARD II TO RICHARD II 33

IV. LANCASTER AND YORK 37

V. EARLY TUDOR 40

VI. ELIZABETH AND JAMES I 45

VII. CHARLES I AND THE COMMONWEALTH . . 49

VIII. CHARLES II TO QUEEN ANNE . . . 52

IX. THE GEORGIANS 55

X. VICTORIAN COSTUME TO 1880 . . . 59

DIAGRAMS 63

LIST OF SUITABLE MATERIALS . . . 158

A SHORT LIST OF BOOKS 159

ILLUSTRATIONS

LISTED CHRONOLOGICALLY

FACING PAGE

1. RICHARD II; FROM THE WILTON DIPTYCH . . 42
2. BANQUET IN LONDON, TEMP. EDWARD IV . *Frontispiece*

FACING PAGE

3. HOLBEIN : THE AMBASSADORS 42
4. PETER OLIVER : SIR THOMAS MORE AND HIS FAMILY 94
5. SWEERTZ : A FAMILY GROUP 54
6. CHARLES II COURT LADY : COUNTESS OF DORSET . 54
7. THE STAGE IN THE EIGHTEENTH CENTURY . . 124
8. HOGARTH : THE GRAHAM CHILDREN . . . 56
9. GAINSBOROUGH : RALPH SCHOMBERG . . . 56
10. EMPIRE PERIOD DAY DRESS 58
11. A MAN OF 1815 : A CARICATURE . . . 58
12. W. P. FRITH : THE RAILWAY STATION . . 60

IN THE TEXT

PAGE

13. SAXON MEN'S COSTUMES 21
14. SAXON WOMAN'S COSTUME 69
15. REGAL COSTUME OF THE TWELFTH CENTURY . 30
16. NORMAN WOMEN'S COSTUMES 76
17. SIDELESS GOWN 80
18. HIGH-WAISTED GOWN 91
19. PROCESSION OF QUEEN ELIZABETH . . . 111
20. CHARLES I MAN 49
21. CHARLES I WOMAN 51
22. GENTLEMEN FROM THE DUKE OF ALBEMARLE'S
   FUNERAL PROCESSION 52
23. A BAR IN LONDON 61
24. GRAND NATIONAL ARCHERY MEETING . . 62

Illustrations 13, 14, 15, 16 and 17 are reproduced by kind
permission from Mrs. Charles Ashdown's *British Costume
during Nineteen Centuries.* (T. Nelson & Sons Ltd.)

DIAGRAMS

	PAGE
SAXON MAN'S SHORT TUNIC	65
SAXON MAN'S LONG TUNIC	67
SAXON WOMAN'S OVER-TUNIC	68
SAXON WOMAN'S GOWN	71
NORMAN WOMAN'S SHORT TUNIC WITH MAUNCH SLEEVE	73
THE JUPON TUNIC	75
THE COTE-HARDIE	78, 79
SIDELESS GOWN	81, 82
SLEEVES : PLAIN, HANGING AND DAGGED	84, 85
FOURTEENTH-CENTURY TUNIC	87
THE HOUPPELANDE	88, 89
HIGH-WAISTED GOWN	92, 93
BAG SLEEVE	94
TUDOR SKIRTED DOUBLET AND TRUNKS	96, 97
TUDOR OVER-GOWN	99
TUDOR WOMAN'S GOWN	100–103
ELIZABETHAN DOUBLET	105
ELIZABETHAN CAPE AND TRUNKS	107
ELIZABETHAN WOMAN'S BELL-SHAPED DRESS	109, 110
CHARLES I MAN'S DOUBLET	113
CHARLES I AND CHARLES II BREECHES	115
CHARLES I LADY'S GOWN	117
CHARLES II MAN'S COAT AND VEST	118, 119
CHARLES II LADY'S GOWN	121
EIGHTEENTH-CENTURY FULL-SKIRTED COAT	123, 124
EIGHTEENTH-CENTURY FULL-SKIRTED WAISTCOAT	125
EIGHTEENTH-CENTURY SQUARE-CUT COAT	127
EIGHTEENTH-CENTURY WAISTCOAT FOR SQUARE-CUT COAT	128
EIGHTEENTH AND NINETEENTH CENTURY BREECHES	129
EIGHTEENTH-CENTURY PANNIER PETTICOAT	131, 132
EIGHTEENTH-CENTURY LADY'S GOWN	134, 135
NINETEENTH-CENTURY CUT-AWAY COAT	137
NINETEENTH-CENTURY WAISTCOAT	138
NINETEENTH-CENTURY MAN'S DICKY SHIRT FRONT	139
NINETEENTH-CENTURY TROUSERS	141
LADY'S EMPIRE GOWN	143
NINETEENTH-CENTURY FROCK-COAT	145
CRINOLINE	147
THE BUSTLE DRESS	149
THE BUSTLE SKIRT	151
HEAD-DRESSES : HOOD, CHAPERONE, TUDOR AND ELIZABETHAN CAPS, GABLE HEAD-DRESS, FRENCH HOOD, HEART-SHAPED HENNIN, AND ELIZABETHAN WINGED CAP	153–157

7

COSTUME DESIGN AND MAKING

INTRODUCTION

I

THIS book is intended as a practical guide to the making of period costumes for stage purposes, but since a minimum of historical knowledge is essential to successful designing, a short historical survey is necessary. For those who wish to study the history of costumes more thoroughly, a short list of the most easily obtained books is appended at the end of this volume.

Before considering the exact shapes of the clothes worn at any given period, some idea of the conditions of life maintaining at that time is necessary, since comfort and practicability have always had a certain influence on fashion. For example, in recent times, the attempt to introduce hobble skirts was more or less abortive, and the fashion lasted only a comparatively short time, as women found that it was impossible to carry on the ordinary everyday business of life with any ease or comfort when their legs were so constricted that it was impossible to step in a carriage or over the gutter without difficulty.

In dealing with the clothing of a primitive period the first consideration is the domestic architecture of the period in relation to the prevailing climatic conditions. This will give the designer an indication as to the heaviness of the material he will need to use for his costumes and also will give him an idea as to the bulkiness of the silhouette at which he must aim, since obviously in cold countries and in primitive times, when the heating of houses was a matter of difficulty, people would have to wear more underclothes in order to keep warm. Except in rare instances a knowledge of the nature and shape of period underclothing is not essential to the designer, since as a rule it is only the outer garments that show, provided that his knowledge is sufficient to enable him to make his designs have the correct outline. It is as well to remember, on this head, that leather was fairly extensively used for under-garments until well on in the eighteenth century. There is mention of a leather petticoat in Queen Anne's wardrobe accounts, and in some memoirs of approximately 1760 there is a description of the clothing supplied to an orphanage in Hertfordshire where the girls were given leather petticoats and leather corsets, which they were obliged to lace tightly.

In the same way, in considering the outdoor clothes of any given period, it is necessary to know, in the case of peasants and artisans, something of the conditions of the wearer's calling, the kind of implements he used for his trade, and the method of employing them ; such things to a certain extent will determine the kind of clothes that he wore and, equally important, the actual way he wore them.

As far as the leisured classes are concerned, for outdoor dress, it is important to know the methods of travel employed at the time with which you are dealing, as these will determine the type of dress. For instance, in the time of Edward II., when most women travelled on horseback, riding astride, the ladies had very full skirts, which gave them ample room to straddle the horse with their skirts tucked under them at the back and still have plenty of skirt left to hang free down each side and preserve the conventions.

This question of travel has another important aspect, since it determines the kind of material it is permissible for the designer to use. For instance, it is quite wrong to use patterned silk material for Saxon costumes, as stuffs of this type were not found in England until a much later date when Crusaders, returning from the Holy Land and Asia Minor, brought with them materials of Saracen origin made of silk patterned with Eastern designs. As facilities for travel became greater, silken materials were imported more freely into England, though probably velvet was not known in this country before the fourteenth century.

It is, of course, impossible to reproduce exactly the materials that were in common use hundreds of years ago, for the methods of weaving were utterly different from those in use to-day even though the principle of warp and woof is basically the same. For instance, it is to-day impossible to obtain a velvet that is similar in texture to the old short-pile velvet of even so recent a date as 1870. The nearest approach to this in modern material is millinery velvet, which has a pile that is equally short, though by no means as close and rich in effect ; but millinery velvet lacks completely the rigidity of Victorian velvet, which did, literally, almost stand by itself. The velvet of 1870 was, of course, machine-made just as is our velvet to-day, but with change of taste in material, except at great cost, it is impossible to repeat the texture of sixty years ago ; how much more impossible therefore is it for us to repeat the texture of materials which were hand-woven. Another difficulty which presents itself to designers is the question of colouring. It is possible to fake the texture of a material to a certain extent by the careful choice of materials and use of linings to give stiffness or weight, but it is impossible to fake colours. Up to about the middle of the nineteenth century all dyes were non-mineral in origin. Since the middle of the nineteenth century all dyes have been aniline, that is, mineral dyes, and now it is impossible to obtain any material in the open market, with the exception of Harris and Donegal tweeds, which are not aniline dyed, with the result that bright colours tend to have a certain crudeness, whilst some colours, such as a clear, cold yellow, are almost impossible to obtain. The old dyes,

though bright, were invariably soft, and therefore a greater
variety of colour combination was possible than is the
case to-day with cruder dyes. It is impossible to give an
accurate description of the difference of quality of colour
obtainable by the old non-mineral dyes. The only safe
method of obtaining a reasonably accurate idea of their
colouring is to visit a good picture gallery and look at
contemporary pictures of the period which you are studying.
This is of course easier in the case of the later periods. It
is fairly easy to get a good idea of the general tone of colour
in vogue at the court of Charles I., for instance, from the
paintings of Van Dyke, but the earlier periods are not so
well served, and here it is necessary to supplement pictures
with the marginal paintings of illuminated manuscripts ;
but in the latter case allowance should be made for the
enamelled texture of the painting, which gives a greater
brilliance than would be possible in dyed materials, though
the quality of the colours is the same. If it is not possible
to pay a visit to the National Gallery or the British Museum
to examine paintings, it is possible to buy accurate post-card
reproductions which will be found to be a great help.

Do not try to take an idea of the colouring or design
of material for any given period from a modern designer.
He can only give his idea of what clothes looked like say
four hundred years ago. A modern painter's idea of what
Henry VIII. looked like, for instance, is of no more help
to a designer than his own, for a modern painter can only
give a twentieth-century idea of what a sixteenth-century
king looked like. If a designer needs a guide, Holbein's
portrait will at least give a sixteenth-century painter's idea
of what a sixteenth-century king looked like, and, since
Holbein was a careful and detailed painter, he will give
a very accurate idea, not only of the colour and texture of
the King's clothes, but also of the pattern in the material,
even down to the design in the gold braid that trims the
King's doublet. Contemporary paintings will also give an
indication of the type of patterns which are permissible in

materials. Pattern designs persist longer than any other form of decoration, and stuffs are still being manufactured which embody the designs that were in use as long ago as the fifteenth century. There is, therefore, no excuse for the designer to be guilty of an anachronism in this respect, especially in the case of the larger patterns. It is admittedly difficult, though not impossible, to repeat the small patterns such as ' thunder and lightning,' ' bird's eye,' ' cross and dot ' of the nineteenth-century prints. Every care should be exercised to avoid the modern geometrical designs for period clothes, as materials patterned in this way are very definitely post-war in date and are known to be so, to almost everybody, so that the use of materials of this type will spoil the historical illusion for even the most ignorant.

II

It is evident that it is impossible for a designer to make actual reproductions of period clothes. All that he is able to do is to create for the spectator the illusion of accuracy. But for the stage designer this is not all, for costumes have, as well as creating the illusion of accuracy, also to be theatrically effective, and be made in a colour combination that will retain its brilliance under stage lighting.

To take the question of theatrical effectiveness first. The designer must realise that he is subordinate to the play, and that in all his efforts he must bear in mind that his costumes must not only be decorative and good in themselves, but must also accentuate the dramatic points of the play as far as possible, and must help to show the characters of the wearers. It would, for instance, be utterly wrong to dress Polonius as a dandy, or Romeo in the habit of a sober merchant. Equally well it would be theatrically ineffective to introduce Mephistopheles in *Faust* dressed in a tender blue when obviously he is intended for the kind of devil who is most at home in a flaming red. To follow out this principle, therefore, the designer must first read the text carefully and get a clear picture in his mind of what the author wished each character to appear ; then he must decide the relative importance of each character in the main business of the plot of the play, and having done that, he must decide which are the most important dramatic points to be accentuated, as these three conditions will determine how he will make up his costume plot.

In assembling his costume plot, the designer should remember that for stage purposes the eye of the spectator is not able to appreciate easily more than about three colours at once, and that therefore to cover his stage with bright shades is defeating his own object. Consideration of a flower-bed full of herbaceous plants all in full bloom, makes one realise how true this is. The general effect is one of extreme brilliance and variety, but this is only achieved as a result of the contrast effected by the background of dark green foliage and brown earth. The designer in the same way must work out his costume plot with a background of negative colouring, and this can best be done by clothing his secondary characters in indeterminate colours with a predominance of one colour in varying shades. Against this background the designer can build up his costume plot for the main characters, his object being so to dress the various people that he can draw the eye of the spectator towards the predominant character in any one of the dramatic scenes which he has already picked out as being of paramount importance in the development of the play. For this it should be remembered that colours in the red-orange-yellow range are more positive—that is, attract the eye more easily—than those in the blue-purple-green range. Pure black and pure and faintly off-white are in a class by themselves, and will be dealt with later. Hot colours—that is, the colours with red in them, red, orange, purple—must be relieved by an intermingling of cold colours, those with blue in them—blue, green, and cold yellow—and *vice versa*, otherwise the effect is intolerable to the eye. If for any reason it is imperative to keep all the costumes in one range, then it is better to choose the blue range, as this is less tiring to look at than the red range. For stage use, however, it is extremely difficult to obtain a good blue, as nearly all the ordinary dyes turn greyish and dirty under even the most careful stage lighting, except where German glass media are used; but as this German glass is extremely expensive and is practically unknown in England, for the present purpose only the ordinary gelatine media need be considered, and with the use of these, blue is proved to be the least successful of all colours for the stage. If it is absolutely essential to use blue, as it is in the case of a Nativity play, for instance, try to obtain a blue with a slight greenish tinge like the ordinary water-colour Prussian blue, as this lights best; but for all ordinary purposes, it is nearly always possible to use varying shades of green to balance your stage colour scheme, where in ordinary circumstances blue would be used. It should always be possible to light any shade of green, except bottle green, which comes up a dirty black, with any ordinary three-circuit lighting plant.

It is obvious that it is an extremely difficult business to build up a completely successful costume plot for a play that is in any way complicated and has numerous characters, but a great deal may be done by the judicious mixture of broken and pure colours. It has already been said that colours in the red range, on the whole, prove stronger than those in the blue range, but this applies to the pure colours. Supposing a mixed red is used—that is, an umber, a pink, or a madder colour—and in opposition to this is put a bright emerald green, then the green, because it is a pure and not a broken colour, will take precedence over the broken-down red. But should a broken-down green be put in opposition to a broken-down red, then the red will tend to be the stronger. It is easy to prove this and to work out combinations of various colours by experimenting with little bits of coloured wools. It is also helpful to carry out the same experiment, using patterns both of silk and of wool, for this will give an idea of the balance that can be achieved by a mixture of textures, since in almost every case a greater brilliance is achieved in the silk than is possible in the wool. We now come to the question of black and white, which are not, properly speaking, colour at all. We have hitherto dealt with the problem of focusing the attention of the audience on any given character by means of dressing that character in the most dominating colour of all those used in any particular scene—that is, we have dressed up to our central character, who has been made the peak of our scheme. But the same effect can be achieved in exactly a reverse manner —that is, we can make our central character stand out from the rest simply by dressing down to him—that is, let all the other characters be brightly dressed, but let the central character be dressed in a completely negative colour. The classic example of this is, of course, Hamlet, who is always dressed in black, whilst the rest of the court is in gay colours. Another Shakespearean example is the modern fashion for dressing King Lear in off-white, and the rest of the characters in fairly positive colours. In modern plays, the most striking example of this method was in the Rickett costumes for *St. Joan*, where all the courtiers wear bright colours, but the Dauphin is dressed very plainly in grey. When employing this method it is necessary to take great care to ensure that the contrast between the brightly coloured costumes and the negative coloured costume of the central character is accentuated by the design of the dresses, as, since it is unnatural for the eye to be attracted to any but the brighter colour, every means must be used to draw it to the desired focal point. It is, of course, obvious that in usual circumstances, when the designer is dressing up his central character, the more important the person the more elaborate the design of the dress, and for servants, peasants, and artisans the designs, not only for historical accuracy but also for correct dramatic effect, must be simple. When the ' dressing-down ' method is used, it will be found to be most effective not only to make the central character negative in colour but also absolutely plain and negative in design, whilst the surrounding characters should be dressed in designs as elaborate and fantastical as the period will allow. Occasionally the demands of the play will necessitate the characters being dressed in colours which will not allow for the proper dramatic balance. Imagine, for instance, a scene between a woman, a man who has to be dressed in black, and a Cardinal whose robes have to be scarlet. The dominance of the scene lies between the man and the woman, and the Cardinal is only of secondary importance. In order not to dominate the man, who has to be dressed in black, the woman must be dressed in white, an equally negative colour, so that the Cardinal is still standing out on the stage like a drop of blood. The only thing that the designer can do in order to correct this is to alter the colour of the Cardinal's robes. They must still be red, because this is the regulation colour, but the shade can be changed from the usual scarlet to a darker colour that will not be so conspicuous, and since there is no other colour at all on the stage with which to compare the brightness of the red, the audience will be unaware that the shade is not as bright as it should be. The result of this change of colour will be that the producer will be able to group his characters so as to draw the attention of the audience where he wants it, rather than having it constantly focused on the Cardinal.

Apart from theatrical effectiveness, there is another consideration when building up a costume plot, and that is to make a colour scheme that is within the range of the lighting plant at your disposal. The most popular lighting combination seems to be blue and amber. This is not very kind to the costume designer, as amber tends to deaden every colour except orange. From the designer's point of view, the best combination is blue and pink, as this will get the best out of most colours, with the exception of orange; but the blue-and-pink combination is not, as a rule, at all popular with the caste, as it necessitates a heavy make-up. It is always a help to the costumes if all light media are frosted, as this diffuses the light and prevents the rather patchy effect that is otherwise inevitable owing to the slight variation in shade as the actor moves from the beam of one light to another. All lighting combinations must be a question of compromise between designer and producer. The general theory is that a blue light will pick up the colour in any costume in the blue range, whilst an amber or a pink will pick up those in the red range. The advantage of the pink over the amber, is that the pink will pick up nearly all the broken colours in the red range whilst the amber will deaden most of them. The designer must, however, limit himself to those colour combinations which it is possible to light. It is not, for instance, possible to light satisfactorily, with a small lighting plant, a colour scheme which comprises blue, pink, and orange. If this is lit with a blue-and-amber combination, the pink will go dead and the blue, unless it is Prussian blue, will turn greyish. If, on the other hand, you use a blue-and-pink combination, the pink will come up well, the blue will come up better than with the amber, but the orange will be killed. With pure white light, of course, any colour scheme can be used, but white light is not very suitable except for ballet and certain types of revue, as it is very hard; but because of this hardness, any colour scheme designed for use under white light should be as bright as possible. There is one colour which is almost unusable except under white light, where it is most effective, and that is a pure vermilion, as it cannot be satisfactorily lit by any lighting combination that will allow for the use of other colours on the stage at the same time. The same effect of brilliance can be achieved by the use of bright scarlet in conjunction with a slight deepening in tone of the other colours employed. Dead white also is not usually very successful as it is too startling—a slight off-white is more effective for the stage.

Richness of effect under stage lighting is achieved by employing mat-surfaced materials such as velvet, satin made of real silk that has a dull sheen for finish, and woollen materials. Brilliance is attained by the use of the lighter silks that have a slightly glossy finish, but these have rather a thin and papery effect from the front, and are only successful for the later periods when depth of texture is not so necessary. Under no circumstances is satin made from artificial silk or cheap cotton sateen successful for stage purposes, as both these materials combine to a very high degree the papery effect of the lighter silks, together with a thorough cheapness and shoddyness of appearance. It is also impossible to make either of these materials retain their freshness for any length of time on the stage.

It is obviously not possible, in a book of this size, to give a comprehensive history of costumes. All that has been attempted is to give a general idea of the type of costume used in any given period between Saxon times and 1880, with a cutting diagram of a representative costume for each period. Many variations of costume other than those given were used, but those given here were most common and are most easily made up. For those who wish to make a further study of the history of costume, a short bibliography is given at the end of the book.

I. SAXON TO NORMAN
460–1066

THE MEN

S AXON costumes, both male and female, are of the simplest possible cut, and depend for effect on the combination of colours used and on careful draping of the mantles and cloaks.

In all classes, and by both sexes, a linen garment was worn next the skin. This linen garment is of importance because it developed into the shirt of the men and the chemisette of the women, that became apparent in later periods. During the Saxon period this linen undergarment was similar in shape to the super-tunic, but except in the case of the poorest peasants, who only possessed one garment, it did not show, as it was covered by the over-tunic. This over-tunic was either about knee-length or, for older persons and formal occasions, down to the ground. A king, for instance, would wear a full-length robe, unless he was hunting or engaged in some other active pursuit, when the shorter tunic would be more suitable.

THE SHORT TUNIC.—This garment was made either from wool or linen material, and reached to the knees. It was cut with only two seams, one up each side, the sleeves being cut in one with the body, in Magyar fashion. In its more primitive form this tunic was without ornamentation, and the neck opening consisted merely of a round hole large enough to allow the passage of the head. By degrees, however, the neck opening became enlarged to a slit extending down the chest, which was joined together by lacing the edges, which frequently were ornamented. Ornamenta-

SAXON MEN'S COSTUMES, SHOWING THE SHORT TUNIC
(*Based on Cott. MS. Tiberius C, vi. British Museum*)

tion was also introduced on the skirt of the tunic. This ornamentation was generally extended up the side seams about half-way up to the waist from the hem, and the seams themselves were left open for about this distance to allow freedom of movement. The ornamentation should either consist of appliquéd pattern in a contrasting colour, plain bands of contrasting colour, or of wool embroidery. Designs are not generally found to be rectangular in form, such as the Greek Key pattern, but are usually rounded. A popular design is either rings or spots, a plain line being embroidered on each side of them so as to form bands; another popular pattern is the four-petalled flower. Sometimes both these designs are used together, and in this case the bands of spots would be used to ornament the neck opening and possibly to make a band round the upper part of the sleeves, midway between the elbow and the shoulder. Ornamentation at the wrist of the sleeves of the men's tunics is unusual, as a distinctive feature of the sleeves of both male and female Saxon dress is the extensive rucking of the sleeve between wrist and elbow, the reason for this apparently being that when the weather was cold, it was possible to pull the sleeve right over the hand for extra warmth. The tunic was held at the waist by a girdle, but this never actually showed, as the tunic was pulled up through it and allowed to blouse over. After violent exercise, the tunic was liable to get pulled through more on one side than the other, giving a lop-sided effect, which was copied by the women.

THE LONG TUNIC OR ROBE.—This was cut in the same Magyar shape as the short tunic, and was worn in much the same way. It was considered a mark of rank and could only properly be worn by persons of importance.

THE MANTLE.—This is an important feature of Saxon dress and took several forms. With the short tunic, either a short cloak can be worn or the longer mantle. The short cloak should be made of a strip of material reaching from about shoulder to waist in depth and of sufficient length to fall in graceful folds in front. Either one or both ends should be rounded, and the fastening can either be made with a brooch, circular in shape and fairly large, or the end of the cloak can be passed through a ring. For stage purposes, however, this latter method is rather clumsy in appearance, and the brooch method is better, but care should be taken in fastening the brooch to gather up the material so that the ends of the cloak fall into straight folds. The neck-opening should be left fairly loose, and the fastening can be made either in front or on the right shoulder, whichever is preferred.

The long mantle, which was worn by both men and women, is more properly worn with the long tunic. It should be full in the skirt and should reach to the ground, the lower hem being rounded. This mantle can also be fastened by a brooch, but in this case the fastening must be made in the centre, as otherwise the long folds of the cloak would make movement difficult and would hamper the use of the arms. If a variation from the use of a brooch is required, the fastening can be made with cords attached to the neck of the mantle. A third type of cloak, but one difficult to manage theatrically, is made from a circular piece of material with a hole made for the head at about three-quarters of the radius so that one side of the material is longer than the other. The longer side forms the back of the cloak, whilst the shorter side is doubled back over the shoulders, making a fold across the throat and leaving the arms free. This can be a decorative garment for tableaux purposes, as the doubled-back fold makes a graceful drapery at each side of the figure, but for ordinary stage purposes it is rather difficult to wear, as movement tends to displace the folds.

LEG COVERINGS.—As a general rule, the Saxons wore knickers, reaching to mid-thigh, which were hidden by the skirts of the tunic; these were either joined by long stockings of cloth, the join also being covered by the skirts of the tunic—which gives the appearance, so common in illustrations of the time, of the men wearing tights—or else by shorter stockings, which stopped below the knee. In the latter case the top of the stocking was usually turned back at a slant, like the top of a Hessian boot. Whichever type of stocking is used, cross-gartering is invariably necessary. This is made from narrow strips of coloured material wound round the calf of the leg in varying patterns, and terminating below the knee. In the case of soldiers this cross-gartering should, properly, be made of strips of leather.

The feet were covered by boots which reached to the ankle. These were sometimes ornamented up the front in the case of the more important people. The leather of which these boots were made seems to have been very soft, and the boots themselves seem to have been of the pull-on type, so that they can be very effectively faked for the stage by the use of socks turned over at the ankle and with soles attached to the feet. These boots were worn by all classes of the people, but the stockings were a feature of the wealthier classes, so that in the case of a peasant costume it would be correct to leave the legs bare from the knee, where the tunic ends, to the top of the boot.

HEAD-DRESS.—As a general rule the Saxons went bareheaded, but the head-dress usually found was in the form of a Phrygian cap, like the French cap of liberty, made of leather or skin, which in the case of the lower classes would have the hair outside, or, in the case of the upper classes, of cloth which was sometimes ornamented. Important personages sometimes wore a cap of a sugar-loaf shape, and this shape was also used for the helmet of the officers, and persisted down to Norman times.

THE WOMEN

THE GUNNA, OR GOWN.—This was a long robe reaching to the ground in ample folds. The sleeves were cut Magyar fashion, and fitted fairly closely to the lower arm, though they show the same characteristic wrinkling as was the case in the sleeves of the men's tunics, being made long enough to pull over the hand in cold weather. The gunna was usually quite plain, but towards the end of the period a band of ornamentation was sometimes introduced at the hem.

THE TUNIC.—This was worn over the gunna, and corresponded roughly to the short tunic of the men. This tunic also reaches about to the knees, is cut Magyar fashion, and has a round neck-opening similar to that in the men's tunic; the variation is found in the sleeves, which reach only to the elbow with a wide bell-shaped opening, and in the ornamentation, which not only occurs round the sleeves and hem and round the neck, but is also continued beyond the neck-opening in front down to the hem. The tunic was worn pulled up through the girdle on the right side in imitation of the men, giving a slanted effect to the hem.

THE HEAD RAIL.—This was a universal head-covering that was worn apparently both indoors and out, and without which no respectable Saxon woman was ever seen. The only illustrations showing women with bare heads are those of doubtful characters, such as dancing-girls. The head rail is a strip of soft material about two and a half yards long and three-quarters of a yard wide. It is adjusted by laying it over the head, with one end reaching to the left shoulder; the length of the material is then passed around the face, under the chin, over the left shoulder, and round the back of the neck. The end can either be left hanging forward over the right shoulder or can be passed under the chin again to hang backwards over the left shoulder. Sometimes the head rail was held in place by a circlet of gold, but this is not essential. Towards the end of the period, however, the circlet became more common, and this resulted ultimately in the head rail being draped loosely over the head, with the ends hanging evenly on each side of the face, the veil being held securely in place by the circlet.

THE MANTLE.—Two types of mantles were worn by women, both similar to those used by the men, and already described in the previous section :

1. The long mantle, fastened by a cord at the throat and hanging in straight folds to the heels.
2. The circular mantle, with the hole cut through which the head was passed. The head rail was worn over this, so that the drapery round the neck hid the opening.

The circular type seems to have been the most common for outdoor use.

GENERAL REMARKS.—Materials suitable for this period are woollen and cloth materials of a plain weave, face cloths and fancy dress materials are not suitable. Colours chosen should be soft dark shades and fairly strong in tone; pastel colours are not permissible. The ornamentation should be in broad bands, and embroidery should be in a bold design. Plain silk materials are suitable for the head rail amongst the upper classes, but linen should be used for the poorer people. The head rail should never be made in white material. During and after the Danish occupation, black became a popular colour.

II. NORMAN TO PLANTAGENET
1066–1307

UNDER William I. there was scarcely any change in costume from that worn during the latter part of the Saxon period. The only variations were the slight shortening of the short male tunic, and also the tightening of the sleeves, which were now made to fit close to the arm, and terminated in a small cuff. Embroidery was used to ornament the hem and neck opening. The short mantle was rather more voluminous than in the preceding period, and frequently worn longer than the tunic. It was fastened either in front or on the shoulder, as before. Head-coverings showed a certain amount of variation— the Phrygian cap and the sugar-loaf cap were still worn; in addition a skull-cap made into a band which came round the forehead, and a flat cap also coming into a band, are both common. The foot-gear remained the same, but boots were now made in various colours instead of the prevailing black of the Saxons.

WILLIAM II, HENRY I, STEPHEN

Under these three kings dress became very much richer and began to show that tendency to exaggeration which was so marked under the later Plantagenets.

THE MEN

The long tunic or ceremonial dress was so lengthened as to reach the ground all round, and the sleeves, which widened at the end, were made so exaggerated as to reach beyond the finger-tips. Rich patterned materials began to be introduced by nobles returning from the first crusade of 1096. After this date pilgrimages to the Holy Land became more frequent, with the result that the importation of Eastern materials was facilitated. This permits a greater range of fabrics for costumes for richer characters. Heavy silks may be used both plain and figured, but care should be taken in the case of figured materials to choose a simple design. If it is not possible to secure a silk of any weight, interlining should be used in order to secure the solid appearance which is correct.

THE SHORT TUNIC was still in use for ordinary everyday wear for the younger men, and, of course, was still worn by the lower classes. Towards the end of this period, on certain occasions when very elaborate dress was worn, the short tunic was worn over the long tunic, both being highly ornamented.

THE MANTLE was worn short or long according to the length of the tunic, and in the case of the nobles was made of the finest cloth and trimmed with fur.

THE CAP was still of a modified Phrygian shape. In bad weather, a cloak was worn with a hood of the Phrygian shape attached.

BOOTS were of the same type, except that the toes became lengthened to a point.

THE WOMEN

THE GOWN was similar to that of the preceding period, except that it was made more tight-fitting at the waist. It was lengthened so as to lie in folds on the ground. The sleeve showed various developments. The over-tunic, which was a customary part of the Saxon woman's dress, was not now invariably worn. When it was absent, the sleeve of the gown was adorned by a long pendant of various types. The simplest form of pendent sleeve was one cut in the fashion of a monk's sleeve, but with the lower point very much elongated, so that it was possible to knot the end—a habit that was very prevalent. Another form of hanging sleeve was that known as the maunch, in which the pendent part took the form of an elongated bag. The maunch sleeve is used in a formalised form in heraldry, and was the sleeve which knights wore as a badge in tournaments, reference to which is familiar to most people from the stories of King Arthur. Ornamentation was introduced to the gown by means of bands of different colour at the hem and at the edges of the pendent sleeves. In cases where the over-tunic was worn, the sleeve of the gown was made tight-fitting to the wrist.

THE OVER-TUNIC was similar to that of the Saxon women, except that it fitted rather less loosely and the short bell-shaped sleeve developed into the pendent type just described.

THE MANTLE remained the same, except that bands of ornamentation are common down each side in the front.

THE HEAD RAIL still was worn, but a slight alteration in its arrangement is found. It was draped over the head by the same method, but the folds were arranged to hang in straight lines on either side, framing the face, and were kept in place by a band, generally embroidered, pulled down on the forehead.

HAIR - DRESSING.—The horror of showing the hair which was felt by the Saxon women does not persist, and women begin to do their hair in two long plaits hanging down each side of the head. These plaits were frequently inserted into long tapering cases which reached nearly to the ground; or where the hair was naturally long, it was plaited with ribbons.

FOOT-GEAR, which rarely shows, owing to the length of the skirts, seems to have remained unchanged.

THE RUSTIC DRESS of both sexes remained the same as during the time of the Saxons.

HENRY II, RICHARD I, JOHN, HENRY III

THE MEN

There is very little variation in dress from the preceding reigns. For ceremonial occasions a new garment was introduced. This was the Dalmatica, which was an over-tunic of ankle length worn over the long tunic and almost completely covering it. This dalmatica was a development of the idea of wearing the short tunic over the long tunic for special occasions, as described in the preceding section. The dalmatica was made either with wide or close-fitting sleeves, was frequently made from figured material, but when plain was generally ornamented by bands of embroidery round the hem, sleeves, and neck. It was cut on the same lines as the long tunic, and was worn with a belt round the hips. The dalmatica was sometimes made to open up the front from the hem.

The other garments remained the same with the exception of THE MANTLE. Though the straight variety which had been in fashion during the preceding reigns still persisted for ceremonial use and for ordinary wear, for travelling there was a reversion to the old alb-shaped circular mantle of the Saxons, only now a hood was attached

REGAL COSTUME OF THE 12TH CENTURY,
SHOWING THE LONG TUNIC, MANTLE, AND
ORNAMENTED BOOTS
(Based on Roy. MS. 2 A, xxii.   British Museum)

to the back of the neck-opening. This HOOD with a short
shoulder cape began as a common head-covering towards
the end of the reign of Henry III., and persisted for a very
long time as the usual head-gear of the lower classes.

The reign of Henry III. was characterised by the rich
materials used for the clothing of the upper classes.

THE WOMEN

The dress of the women remained substantially the same as in the preceding reigns.

THE GOWN became rather more close-fitting, though it still fell in ample folds to the ground, the fullness starting from the waist. The sleeves were long and tight-fitting to the arm from elbow to wrist, the long wrist-opening being fastened by buttons. The gown, though of the same type, was made lower in the neck. The opening was circular, the line of the neck being low enough to show the collar-bones in front. The lower neckline allowed the linen under-tunic worn next the skin, which hitherto had been hidden by the high neckline of the robe, to show. The neck of the under-tunic was gathered up round the base of the throat, and frequently was fastened with a brooch in front. The gown was enclosed at the waist by a belt with a long end hanging down in front. The waist was low.

THE TUNIC.—This showed the same development as the over-tunic of the men—that is, it was lengthened to just above the hem of the gown. The long pendent sleeves of the preceding reign quite disappeared and the tunic was made sleeveless. This over-tunic was not a necessary part of the costume of the period, the gown frequently being worn alone.

THE MANTLE continued the same as in the preceding reigns.

THE HEAD RAIL.—This showed a definite development, the veil passing over the head was shortened so that it only hung down in straight folds on either side of the face, the ends reaching to the shoulders. In order to cover the throat, a second piece of material was passed under the chin and fastened on top of the head by a brooch or by tying —this second piece of material being worn under the veil.

These two pieces of material together came to be known as the wimple head-dress. This head-dress was frequently white, but towards the end of this period yellow seems to have become a very favourite colour for it. The wimple completely hid the hair, and the bound plaits seen in the ceremonial dress of the preceding reigns now were only worn by queens, whilst the ordinary people and the nobles reverted to the old prejudice against showing the hair.

FOOT-GEAR remained the same.

As in the case of the men, materials became increasingly rich, especially during the reign of Henry III.

EDWARD I

Clothing for both sexes remained substantially the same as it had been in the preceding reigns. The hood which had begun to be used at the end of Henry III.'s reign now became the usual head covering and remained in use in the lower classes until the time of the Tudors. Women varied the method of arranging the wimple in order to imitate the chain mail hoods of the men. A band of embroidery was frequently used to hold the veil in place. The narrow sleeve of the men's tunics and of the women's robes were now regularly fastened by four buttons placed between wrist and elbow. The gowns of the women developed in length in this reign until they lay in folds on the ground both in front and at the back.

III. EDWARD II TO RICHARD II

1307–1399

EDWARD II

THE MEN

THIS reign shows a definite change in costume.

THE JUPON TUNIC.—The tunic became more close-fitting to the body, until it was tight down to a level with the hips. It was fastened from neck to hip line with large buttons down the front. At the hips a full skirt reaching to the knee was added. This skirt had no apparent fastening, but was voluminous enough to allow the edges to overlap in front; it was frequently made of a contrasting colour to the body of the tunic.

THE COURT PIE.—In cold weather the jupon tunic was covered by a development of the old Saxon circular cloak—called the Court Pie. This garment was always made in two contrasting colours and was of three-quarter length. It was a circular garment with an opening in the centre for the head. It was cut in two semicircles of contrasting colours, and worn with the join in the centre back and front.

THE HOOD was the usual form of head-covering and showed a development of the peak at the back. This was elongated into a long tab which hung down the back as far as the waist, and was called a liripipe. The liripipe was either left hanging or was wound round the neck or round the crown of the head, giving a turban-like appearance.

GLOVES came into fashion at this date among the upper classes, and BELTS, worn round the hips, became more and more ornate.

THE WOMEN

There was not the same development in women's dress in this reign as there was in that of the men. Women still dressed in robes of an excessive length. Sometimes an under-robe with tight sleeve and fitting close round the neck is shown under a loose over-robe worn without a girdle and with loose three-quarter sleeves and low boat-shaped neck line. When the over-robe is worn it is frequently ornamented by bands of contrasting shades round the neck line and ends of the sleeves. The wimple head-dress was still used, but the hair was allowed to show a little round the face. Aprons, without bibs, and reaching to about the knee, were in use.

EDWARD III

THE MEN

For the first half of this reign costumes remained practically the same as in the preceding reign. The jupon tunic was still in use, the only innovation being the introduction of a long pendant, attached above the elbow, and known as a tippet. The tippet was made of white material and was worn either plain or dagged. Dagging—that is, scalloping of the edge of a garment—became very fashionable in this reign and was frequently very elaborate. Parti-coloured tunics were also fashionable. Hoods with increasingly long liripipes were worn, and in this reign the cape part of the hood was frequently lengthened to reach over the shoulders. Mantles were worn, reaching to ankle-length at the back but with the lower edge rounded so that, at the front opening, the sides of the mantle only reached to just below the knee. The belt, worn round the hips, was highly ornamented and frequently had a sporran-shaped pouch hanging from it. Towards the end of this reign the sleeves of this tunic were lengthened until the cuff reached over the knuckles.

THE WOMEN

THE COTE-HARDIE.—The gowns of the women remained substantially the same in outline as in the preceding reign, though, like the clothing of the men, they became more close-fitting. They were cut with a close-fitting bodice reaching to the hips and a full circular skirt, which was long enough to lie in folds on the ground.

The join of the bodice and skirt was frequently covered by a belt. The sleeves were long and close-fitting, with a row of buttons between elbow and wrist. The sleeve itself, towards the end of the reign, was lengthened so that the cuff reached over the knuckles. The tippet pendant was also attached to the sleeves of women's gowns, but in their case the tippet was extended to the ground. Mantles were worn, reaching the ground in length and fastened with cords at the neck.

RICHARD II

THE MEN

This reign was distinguished by the introduction of a new garment which was to prove popular for the next three reigns. This garment was the HOUPPELANDE. It was a long coat-like garment, sometimes made open all the way down the front and sometimes with a neck-opening only. It was never made shorter than half-way up the calf of the leg, and frequently, especially for ceremonial wear, was made right down to the ground with a long train. It was held in at the waist by a belt. The collar was high and fastened under the chin. The sleeves showed considerable variations. They could be either close-fitting or wide. The wide sleeve was frequently dagged, as was also the hem in the shorter type of houppelande.

THE STRAIGHT TUNIC.—This was merely a development of the jupon tunic without the skirt. It was fairly close-fitting, usually with a high collar, and showed the same variations of sleeve as the houppelande. It was worn with a belt round the hips.

THE CHAPERONE.—This form of hat, which came into use during this reign, was one of the most decorative forms of head-gear ever worn in England. It consisted of a head-band about 2 inches wide, to which was attached a frill of material about 12 inches deep, the edge of which was frequently dagged. A long liripipe was used to bind it in position.

FOOT-GEAR.—During this reign, shoes began to show exaggeratedly long-pointed toes—but for stage purposes these are not practical, as they make walking difficult; but foot-gear at this period should show a sharp point.

THE WOMEN

The fashion for the cote-hardie and mantle still prevailed in this reign, and an over-robe was added, though this was not invariably worn. This over-robe was known as the Sideless Gown. The bodice of the sideless gown was sleeveless, and the armholes were made of such exaggerated size that they reached from shoulder to hip, so that the bodice was, literally, sideless. The neck of the bodice was cut low to show the cote-hardie underneath, and the front panel of the bodice was narrow. The bodice was cut hip-length, and to it was attached a long, full, circular skirt.

THE CRESPINE HEAD-DRESS.—This consisted of a coronet about 2 inches or 3 inches deep, at each side of which were attached cauls, cylindrical cases in which to confine the hair. The cauls reached from the base of the coronet to the angle of the jaw, concealing the ears. Both coronet and cauls should be rich in appearance and decorated with jewels. Since nowadays most people wear their hair short, the cauls can be made solid, but it is essential that they should be so attached to the coronet that they fit close to the face. A veil should be attached to the coronet at the back to conceal the back of the head. Wide gold braid backed with canvas forms a good coronet, and the cauls may be made from bags of gold net stuffed out with a roll of material to imitate coils of hair.

IV. LANCASTER AND YORK
1399-1485

HENRY IV, HENRY V, HENRY VI

THE MEN

THERE was practically no change during these three reigns in the costume of the men except that bag sleeves became popular. This sleeve was made tight at wrist and armhole, but otherwise was voluminous, and hung in a deep pouch. Baldricks dagged at the lower edge and hung with bells were also worn at this date. Dagging of sleeves and hem of the houppelande began to go out of fashion.

THE WOMEN

The same fashions as those of Richard II. still prevailed, but a new type of gown, the high-waisted, was added. This was worn with a mantle but without the cote-hardie.

THE HIGH-WAISTED GOWN consisted of a close-fitting bodice cut very short-waisted, fitting closely, and with a V-neck. The skirt was long in front and extended to a train at the back. The sleeves were tight-fitting. The junction of skirt and bodice was disguised by a wide belt.

THE HEART HEAD-DRESS.—This was a development of the crespine. The cauls became enlarged until finally they reached above the coronet, and gradually the shape of the whole crespine changed, so that instead of the cauls being pendent they stood above the head. The hair, however, was still concealed.

EDWARD IV, EDWARD V, RICHARD III

THE MEN

During the reign of Edward IV. the Houppelande, though still worn, began to go out of fashion for younger and smarter men, and the short straight tunic became more popular. This showed a certain development in fullness, though in general idea it remained the same garment. In cutting the straight tunic for this period, an extra 4 inches width should be allowed on back and front beyond that shown in the cutting diagram to allow for the loose pleats back and front which were characteristic. Padding should also be added under the shoulder seams in order to give a square broad-shouldered effect. The neck of the tunic was cut lower and rounded, to show the shirt underneath. The dagged sleeve was no longer in use, but the bag sleeve was still popular. A development of the bag sleeve, a long cylindrical-shaped bag, cut square at the bottom, became extremely popular. This cylindrical bag sleeve did not fulfil the functions of a sleeve at all, as it did not cover the arm but was merely pendent from the back of the shoulder. It was sometimes allowed to hang down on each side, and sometimes the sleeves were loosely tied together at the back. This type of bag sleeve was worn with close-fitting inner sleeves. Another form of sleeve was the CUT SLEEVE. This consisted of two pieces of sleeve joined together by lacing, the undershirt showing through. This is an economical form of sleeve if material is getting short. It is most easily made by cutting a tight-fitting sleeve to reach to the elbow, and a second close-fitting piece of sleeve to fit the lower arm from elbow to wrist. The two halves are joined together by lacing at the elbow.

HATS showed some variation at this date. Small, close-fitting round caps with a long plume worn at the side or front were worn, also plain sugar-loaf brimless felt hats and a brimmed type of felt hat known as the Bicocket. This was a sugar-loaf-shaped crown of one colour with a brim of a different colour rolled at the back and projecting in a long peak in front. It was trimmed with a long feather.

THE WOMEN

There was no change in women's dress except that the high-waisted gown became even shorter in the waist and was cut lower in front.

A new head-dress was introduced at this period called the HENNIN. This was a tall, pointed cone like a dunce's cap, about 2 feet high, which can easily be made from buckram covered with thin silk. It had a band of velvet about 2 inches to 3 inches wide sewn across the front, with each end hanging down each side of the face to the level of the angle of the jaw. A long veil was attached to the top of the hennin at the back. This head-dress should be worn at an angle of 45 degrees, and is extremely difficult to keep on owing to the weight of the veil at the back. It will probably be found necessary to wear it with an elastic under the chin. This can be disguised fairly well by the side pendants of the velvet head-band.

V. EARLY TUDOR
1485–1558

HENRY VII

THIS reign shows the transition from medieval costume to what we have come to regard as Tudor costume proper.

THE MEN

Definite development was shown in every garment during this reign. The Houppelande, now used as an over-gown, took on the peculiarities of a loose coat. It was open down the front but had no fastenings. It was worn either full length, belted at the waist, or knee length, when it was allowed to hang free. The length was determined chiefly by the age and importance of the wearer. The collar, which in the time of Richard II. had been high and closed, was now found in the form of wide lapels as if it had been left open and allowed to fall back on the shoulders. The sleeves were either of the cylindrical bag type, or else loose and wide at the wrist; this latter type was usually found on the full-length gown.

THE TUNIC now was made close-fitting to the waist, where it sometimes had a short basque attached; sometimes it stopped at the waist. It was cut with a long V in front reaching to the waist, and was laced over the shirt or over an ornamented stomacher. The sleeves were either close-fitting or cut and laced according to the fashion which began to be popular in the preceding period.

FOOT-GEAR.—The pointed-toed shoes which had been popular since the time of Richard II. went out of fashion and were succeeded by a wide-toed type that ultimately developed into the spatulate shoe of the Tudors. Knee-high boots of soft leather also became popular.

THE CHAUSSES, or tights, which had been in use for generations, now began to disappear and were succeeded by tight-fitting breeches and hose. These breeches ended about mid-thigh and were frequently parti-coloured or striped, as were the hose.

HEAD-GEAR.—The close-fitting round cap of the preceding period was still popular. An innovation was the SQUARE CAP which prevailed as a head-dress for clerks and lawyers for a long time, and which is still worn by the women undergraduates at Oxford. In its simplest form the square cap is made from two squares of material joined together round the edge ; a circular hole is cut in one square for the head. The head-opening is finished by a head-band 1 inch deep. The cap should be worn with one point facing forward.

THE WOMEN

The high-waisted gown still persisted, but was now either cut square at the neck or left open in a V from the waist upwards and laced over a stomacher. The sleeves were no longer tight-fitting, but were either loose bishop's sleeves drawn into a band at the wrist or the cut sleeve, both forms showing the influence of the predominant male fashions. The Chemise is shown frequently drawn up round the neck, and the chemise sleeve shows through the lacing of the cut sleeve. The skirt of the gown was worn shorter in front, but this was compensated for by the additional length of the train, which was frequently long enough to be worn turned up and tucked into the belt at the back.

HEAD-DRESS.—The head-band of the Hennin gradually grew longer and wider until finally it was below the shoulder on each side, whilst the peak of the Hennin became smaller and smaller until finally it disappeared altogether and was replaced by a hood. This form of head-dress became known as the KENNEL, and it was popular also during the next reign. A cutting diagram and illustration of it are given.

HENRY VIII

THE MEN

THE OVER-GOWN, which had developed from the houppelande in the last reign, now became an almost universal garment for all serious men, though a young man might dispense with it. It was knee length, and full in the skirt, being pleated on to a yoke. It was worn open in front and had a deep square collar, frequently of fur. It was sometimes sleeveless, sometimes worn with a full puff sleeve reaching half-way down the upper arm. For old men and members of the clerical professions this over-gown was sometimes extended to the full length as it had been worn in the preceding reign.

THE DOUBLET.—This was made close-fitting to the waist, and had a straight basque or skirt, reaching to just above the knee, pleated on to it. The junction of bodice and basque was concealed by a belt or a piece of ribbon tied round the waist. The habit of showing the shirt under the doublet, which had become fashionable in the cut sleeves of the previous reign, now became very much accentuated. This is shown in the lavish slashes cut in the doublet bodice and in the sleeves, through which the shirt was pulled in little puffs. The neck of the doublet was often finished with a collar band about 1 inch high, though sometimes it ended merely in a close-fitting circular opening without the band. The shirt, however, was finished with a collar band surmounted by a narrow ruff frill about 2 inches wide which showed above the neck of the doublet. If the sleeves were plain they were slashed generously throughout their length, and this type would be worn with the sleeved gown. Sometimes, however, the sleeves were made with a generous puff reaching to just above the elbow, and the lower part only was plain and slashed. This type would be worn with the sleeveless over-gown. The doublet was fastened down the front from neck to waist.

RICHARD II   *From the Wilton Diptych, The National Gallery*
The Houppelande: Note high collar and hanging sleeve

HOLBEIN: THE AMBASSADORS   *The National Gallery*
Note the two types of over-gown, and the square cap worn by the
man on the right

Breeches were worn under the doublet, but rarely showed, as they were short and the skirts of the doublet usually covered them. The lower part of the leg was covered by hose. For modern stage use tights are found more satisfactory than stockings, as they are more easily prevented from wrinkling.

Shoes were of the square-toed spatulate type worn in the preceding reign, but the passion for slashing was also shown here, the upper part of the shoe being slashed across the toe and the slashes puffed with bright-coloured material.

Hats.—The square cap of the preceding reign was still worn by the old men and the clerical professions. For general use the prevailing form of head-gear was the Flat Cap, which was shaped like a large-brimmed tam-o'-shanter. This was worn with a short plume attached between crown and brim.

Male attire during this reign was characterised by its extreme richness. Gold and silver braid was used lavishly and the ends of the doublet slashings were frequently ornamented by jewels.

THE WOMEN

The high-waisted gown which had been popular for so long still persisted with certain variations. It was now cut square at the neck, and worn open in front over a petticoat, the skirt at the back having a long train. The sleeves, which previously were more or less close-fitting, now were made long and pendent, and were turned back in a deep cuff reaching the whole length of the forearm and showing a contrasting lining frequently made of fur. Under this wide turned-back sleeve an inner sleeve was worn of almost uniform pattern. It was usually white and full, but gathered into a narrow band to fit the wrist. Above this white full sleeve there were six bands of strapping joining at the wrist and being caught at intervals up the arm by jewels stitched between the strappings. The white sleeve was pulled through the strappings to form puffs.

HEAD-DRESS.—The KENNEL head-dress described in the preceding reign still persisted, but after the divorce of Catherine of Aragon slight modifications crept in, until at the end of Henry VIII.'s reign the FRENCH HOOD became more usual. The French hood consisted of a halo-shaped piece standing away from the face, with a long bag at the back concealing the hair. This bag was usually worn doubled back against the head and pinned. A cutting diagram and illustration of this head-dress is given.

THE POORER PEOPLE

A definite change from the straight tunic and straight robe of the peasants is now found.

The men wore a doublet made on the same lines as that of the nobleman, but of plain material and without slashing. The flat cap without the feather became the usual headgear, although the hood was still sometimes worn.

The women now wore gowns cut more on the lines of those worn by rich women—that is, square at the neck and open over a petticoat in front, but the sleeves were close-fitting and the neck line higher. Aprons were worn at this time. The head-dress for the poorer women was a coif. This was a close-fitting cap made after the fashion of a baby's bonnet, but without the strings. Coifs were also worn by old men, very often under their hats, and also were used as night-caps.

EDWARD VI AND MARY

There was practically no change in costume during these reigns beyond a modification of the sleeve of the women's gowns. These were no longer made with the long hanging cuff turned back. The sleeve was now made in the form of a full bishop's sleeve, gathered into the wrist and slashed its whole length at the front and back of the arm. These slashes, through which showed the sleeve of the chemise, were caught at about three intervals up the arm, the joins being marked by jewels.

VI. ELIZABETH AND JAMES I
1558–1625

ELIZABETH

THE MEN

THE DOUBLET was now made fairly close-fitting, but the waist line, instead of being straight, was dropped to a definite peak in front. The doublet was frequently padded, and small slashings, known as pinking, were cut both in the body and the sleeves. The long pleated basque of the time of Henry VIII. quite disappeared, and was superseded by a narrow basque, cut on the cross, which stood out sideways over the breeches, or trunks, which now became visible. The sleeves lost the puff which had been familiar in the preceding period. They were made leg of mutton in shape, frequently padded, and sometimes, when not pinked, were slashed down the outside to show the shirt. In this case the slashings were caught in two or three places by jewels, as had been the case of the women's sleeves in the reign of Queen Mary. A long epaulette or roll was usually added at top of the sleeve and a small ruffle was worn at the wrist. The neck of the doublet was finished with a band about 1 inch to 2 inches high, over which appeared the ruffled neck of the shirt. This neck ruffle gradually increased in size and, after the introduction of starch to England about the year 1564, sometimes assumed exaggerated proportions. The large ruff was a separate garment and not part of the shirt.

THE OVER-GOWN had now gone out of fashion except for old men and serious characters. It was used in its full-length form and remained the same as in the reign of Henry VIII. For general use the over-gown was superseded by the cape. This was a short circular cape reaching only to the hips. It was worn slung down the back and slightly over one shoulder. It was usually made with a high standing collar.

THE BREECHES, OR TRUNKS.—These now showed, and were a very definite feature of Elizabethan dress. They were made enormously wide and puffed, but were gathered in to fit the leg at about mid-thigh. They were frequently ornamented by strappings.

SHOES.—These were more or less of the same type as those of Henry VIII., but the spatulate shape was not so exaggerated and the slashings were replaced by a rosette. Boots also were worn.

HATS.—These showed some variation. The square cap still persisted for sober characters, and the flat cap, now made without a brim, was also popular. In addition, a tall-crowned felt hat with a narrow brim was popular. This was worn with a bunchy plume in front.

THE WOMEN

The development in the dress of the women showed the same features as that of the men. The gown was still made opening over a petticoat in front, but the waist line was allowed to drop to a point in front, giving a long-waisted effect; and the stomacher, which now became generally used, accentuated this. The sleeves were frequently made in the leg-of-mutton shape used for the men, in which case they were ornamented by a wide epaulette or roll at the shoulder, or else they were tight fitting from the wrist to half-way up the upper arm where a small puff was added ; small ruffs were worn at the wrist. The neck-opening was square. In some cases the neck-opening was filled in by a yoke known as a Partlet, which fitted close up to the neck, and which was worn with a ruff. The partlet is not, however, a necessary part of the costume. It is more usually found in the costume of citizens' wives, when it is frequently highly ornamented. With this gown ruffs at first were worn, but towards the end of the reign these began to be displaced by high Medici collars which were made on a wire frame. The ruff, however, did not entirely disappear. The skirt of the gown was straight without a train.

THE FARTHINGALE.—This was a crinoline petticoat worn underneath the petticoat proper, and used to extend the skirts to a desired shape. This is the first time that a framework of the kind is used. The farthingale gradually came into use at the accession of Elizabeth, persisted into the reign of James I., and gradually died out again by the time of Charles I. In its original form it was bell-shaped. The bell farthingale is made from two widths of sheeting 48 inches wide and about 42 inches long. Join the two widths together along the selvedges. Face back the top and bottom with inch tape. Stitch a row of tape to take crinoline wire all round skirt at equal intervals, so that, including the hem facing, there are four rows of tape for wire in all. Run wire through the four tapes, graduating the circumference of the wires so as to make the petticoat in the shape of a bell with a slightly fluted mouth; this is obtained by making the wire at the hem quite definitely larger than those higher up.

Towards the end of the reign this form began to die out, and the ring at the top of the petticoat began to be extended. Finally, only two rings were used, one about 9 inches from the waist and the other at the hem. Both these rings were the same size. This later form was called the wheel or ring farthingale, and a slight modification of the gown marked its use; whereas with the bell farthingale the skirt of the gown had been pleated on to the bodice quite plainly, with the introduction of the ring farthingale, a frill of material was added at the waist known as a waist ruff. This was made of the same material as the gown, was about 9 inches deep, and was pleated on to the bodice above the skirt. When worn, the waist ruff should reach to the rim of the top hoop of the ring farthingale, and from this point the skirt should fall perpendicularly.

HEAD-DRESS.—Head-dresses were not invariably worn during the Elizabethan period. The prejudice against showing the hair no longer existed, and as the Queen was very proud of hers it became quite usual for the head to be bare indoors. One form of cap which is very becoming, however, is the Elizabethan wing cap, a development of the Mary Stuart cap, a diagram for which is given.

To MAKE A RUFF.—1 yard organdie 36 inches wide is required. Cut the organdie into ¼-yard strips and join selvedge to selvedge. Double this strip over to make a strip 4½ inches wide, and press. Double this strip backwards and forwards in pleats 2 inches wide, and press lightly. Hold pleated strip in left hand with raw edges facing towards left and folded edges towards right. Stitch together the top and second pleats at a point about ½ inch from the top. Then stitch together second and third pleats at a point about ½ inch from the bottom, and so on until the end of the strip is reached. Back the raw edges of the ruff with a piece of 2-inch tape of a length to fit the neck of the wearer. Fasten with hooks and eyes at neck and press-stud at outside of ruff.

THE PEASANTS wore the same type of clothing as that of the nobles, except that materials and cut were as plain as possible. Peasants did not wear ruffs, but the plain turn-down collar or small frill of the skirt showed above the doublet. The women wore similar costumes to those of the court ladies but of plain material, and in the case of the poorer classes the Partlet was worn, whilst the hair was covered with a coif. Aprons were worn. Farthingales were not used by the lower classes.

JAMES I

There was no substantial change in costume during this reign. Men's breeches gradually became longer, and the bell farthingale was entirely superseded by the ring variety.

VII. CHARLES I AND THE COMMONWEALTH
1625–1660

CHARLES I

THE MEN

THE doublet still remained close-fitting, with the waist drooping to a peak in front, but it was no longer padded. The basque was lengthened and divided into six or eight lapels, the two in centre front and at the centre back being longer and pointed. The sleeves still retained the leg-of-mutton shape, but were either slashed from top to bottom, the slashes being left open, or were very

CHARLES I MAN
From ' The English Dancing Master,' No. 42, by Playford, 1651. British Museum

49

heavily strapped, in which case the slashes were omitted. Turned-back cuffs of point lace were worn at the wrists and a deep square collar edged with point lace was worn at the neck. The front of the doublet was trimmed with buttons, and knots of ribbons decorated the waist. The lapels were frequently edged with braid.

THE BREECHES remained full, but were lengthened to below the knee, where knots of ribbon were worn.

THE CLOAK was lengthened until it reached half-way down the thigh. It was made without a collar.

SHOES remained similar to those of the preceding two reigns. The toes were square and were decorated with rosettes. Boots with wide turned-down tops were also used.

HATS.—These were of felt, high in the crown and wide in the brim which was cocked on one side. They were trimmed with flowing plumes. The men wore their hair in long ringlets.

THE WOMEN

For the first time the gown was made in two parts— bodice and skirt. The Farthingale was no longer used. The bodice was cut with a square neck, fairly low in front ; the waist was lapelled as in the doublet of the men, but in the case of the women the lapels were cut square and were of even length, reaching to hip level. The sleeves were short, finishing above the elbow, and puffed, and they were worn with a turned-back cuff of point lace. A deep collar of lawn edged with point lace was worn at the neck. The bodice was worn outside the skirt, with a sash of ribbon about 2 inches deep round the waist tied in a knot at the side.

THE SKIRT.—This was full and pleated on to a waist band. It reached the ground all round and had no front opening.

The hair was worn dressed in ringlets and without a cap. THE PEASANTS AND POORER PEOPLE wore costumes of the same type but without ornamentation and without such extensive lapelling at the waist. The lapels in the men were confined to two, with the opening at the centre front and back. These lapels reached about mid-thigh. In place of the lace collars and cuffs, plain linen was used both for men and women. Coifs made with the part framing the face sufficiently wide to turn back, and aprons were worn by the women. Hats for both sexes were high in the crown and wide and straight in the brim, and were trimmed with a plain band and buckle. The men wore their hair short.

THE PURITANS.—Their dress was that of the poorer class, and was characterised by sombreness of colouring—brown, black, or grey being usual.

COMMONWEALTH.—Dress was as above.

CHARLES I WOMAN
From an engraving by Hollar

VIII. CHARLES II TO QUEEN ANNE
1660–1714

CHARLES II.

THE MEN

A T the Restoration the men wore a fantastic form of
dress, with short waist-length jackets over a full
shirt which pouched out round the waist. The jacket had
short sleeves and was
adorned with tabs of
ribbon wherever pos-
sible. The sleeves of
the shirt were full, and
ended at the wrist with
a lace ruffle.

CHARLES II MEN
*From ' The Crocodile of Knights, Gentlemen,
etc,' in the Funeral Procession of the Duke
of Albemarle. British Museum*

T H E B R E E C H E S,
known as PETTICOAT
BREECHES, were full
and loose at the bot-
tom, giving the appear-
ance of a petticoat; they
reached to just above
the knee. Sometimes an
actual petticoat was
worn over a pair of
short breeches of the
old plus-four type which
ended in a deep ruffle
of lace.

THE CLOAK was
similar to that of the
preceding reign.

Boots ended below the knee, and had wide turned-back tops which were filled with a lace ruffle.

This style only persisted for about six years, after which Charles II. introduced a more sober type of dress which has persisted with variations until our own day. This consisted of a—

COAT, cut perfectly plain, and reaching to the knees. The side and centre back seams were left open to hip-level to allow room for movement. The sleeves were short at the elbow and terminated in a deep turned-back cuff. A pocket without a flap was cut out in each front lapel, very low down. Shoulder-knots of ribbon of a contrasting colour were worn on each shoulder.

WAISTCOAT.—This was of the same length as the coat, and perfectly plain in cut, ornamented only with a row of buttons down the front. It was sometimes made from figured material.

BREECHES were of the plus-four type, worn with knots of ribbon at the knee. The breeches, with the exception of the knee-knots, were almost completely hidden by the coat and vest.

HATS were low in the crown and wide in the brim. They were sometimes worn cocked and trimmed with trailing plumes.

CRAVATS, trimmed with lace, were worn for the first time. A cravat is a straight piece of linen about 6 inches wide, and long enough to pass twice round the neck and to be tied in front by looping one end over the other so that the lace ruffles at the ends fall one above the other, reaching to the chest.

SHOES were square-toed and trimmed with buckles. At this period shoe heels began to be painted red.

WIGS.—Full-bottomed periwigs were worn.

THE WOMEN

The gown was again made as one garment, and the lapelled bodice of the preceding reign disappeared. The skirt was sometimes divided in front over a petticoat often made of the same material, but ornamented with lace and ribbons. The skirt of the gown sometimes, but not always, had a train at the back. The bodice was rounded and cut very low, showing the chemise which also was cut low. The sleeves of the gown were short, full, and slashed. The sleeves of the chemise were very full and puffed, the extent of the puff being sufficient to distend the sleeve of the gown and show through the slashing. Towards the end of the period tapes were attached to the sides of the front opening and to the side seams of the skirt of the gown, that, when tied, looped the gown back and bunched it over the hips. The hair was worn bare.

THE LOWER CLASSES wore clothing of the same type, but without the ornamentation. The men wore plain white neck-cloths without lace. The gowns of the women were not looped back. Aprons were worn and the mob cap began to take the place of the coif. The front of the gown was sometimes left open and laced over the chemise. Sometimes a corset was worn laced over the gown in front.

JAMES II, WILLIAM AND MARY, ANNE

There was no substantial change in costume during these reigns beyond the introduction of the Tower head-dress for women. This was a round lace cap fitting over the head and confining the hair, to the front of which was attached a starched and pleated piece of lace reaching across the front of the head and attaining a height of about 12 inches from the top of the head in front, though it was slightly lower at the sides. A ribbon passed across the front of this at the bottom, and hung in pendants on each side of the face, reaching to the shoulders. Aprons made of lace also became extremely fashionable.

CHARLES II COURT LADY
Mary Crompton, Countess of Dorset.
(*After Kneller*)

SWEERTZ: A FAMILY GROUP
A Puritan family—the mother and children wear coif caps

IX. THE GEORGIANS
1714–1837

GEORGE I, GEORGE II

THE MEN

THE straight coat that had prevailed from the time of Charles II. gradually went out of fashion and was replaced by what is known as the FULL-SKIRTED COAT. This was the same length as the straight coat, but the skirts were very much flared so that they fluted out at the sides and back. The waistcoat worn under this coat also showed the same tendency, being cut wide at the bottom of the skirt in front. The sleeves of the coat were still short and terminated with a cuff, leaving the shirt sleeve showing from elbow to wrist. The cuffs of the shirt were finished with lace ruffles which hung over the hand. A laced cravat was worn round the neck. The breeches were no longer worn in the baggy plus-four shape but were made to fit close to the knee. Stockings were worn pulled up over the breeches and the tops turned down in a roll above the knee. Shoes were buckled. For riding, boots were worn. Hats were now three-cornered in shape, worn with a peak in front. The full-bottomed wig began to go out of fashion, and the hair was worn tied back and frequently powdered.

THE WOMEN

The skirts were no longer looped back, but the widening of the silhouette at the hips, which was attained by the looping of the skirts, still prevailed but was achieved by a hooped under-petticoat which was worn flat in front and at the back and extended at the sides. The skirt was still worn open in front over an under-skirt, and beneath this under-skirt the hooped petticoat was worn. The neck of the gown was cut low and square in the front and was frequently worn with a fichu. The sleeves were straight and short, and were finished with a ruffle of lace falling down the arm. The hair was worn without a head-dress and was powdered. Patches were worn on the face. Jewellery, chiefly diamonds, was popular.

THE LOWER CLASSES wore the same type of dress as the courtiers, but made of plainer material and without the lace—plain linen being used in its place. The women wore mob caps. The hooped petticoat was not worn by the poorer women.

THE PEASANTS.—The men wore smocks over their breeches, coloured neckcloths knotted round their necks, and slouch hats. The women were dressed as the lower class of townswomen.

GEORGE III

THE MEN

THE full-skirted coat went out of fashion and was superseded by the SQUARE-CUT COAT. This coat was slightly shorter than the Full-Skirted Coat. A standing neckband was added, about 2 inches high. It was worn with a waistcoat which also was cut much shorter, approaching the length of a modern waistcoat. The breeches, shoes, and hat remained the same as in the preceding reign.

By about 1780 the fronts of the square-cut coat began to be sloped back more and more, rather after the fashion of a modern morning coat. The neckband developed into a roll collar. By the end of the century the tendency to push the skirts of the coat further and further back had finally produced a new type of coat, the CUTAWAY. This coat ended at the waist in front, but had tails at the back.

HOGARTH : THE GRAHAM CHILDREN   *The National Gallery*
Except that the gowns are not opened over underskirts, these dresses are typical of the
day costume of an eighteenth-century lady

GAINSBOROUGH : RALPH SCHOMBERG
The National Gallery
George III square-cut coat

The modern evening tail-coat is a survival of the Cutaway of the early nineteenth century. The coat was made double-breasted, and could be fastened or not as required. The waistcoat was also cut short, finishing at the waist. The breeches remained the same, but the stockings were worn underneath instead of over the breeches. Pumps were worn in place of the buckled shoes, and hessian boots became popular. The tricorn hat was replaced by a beaver with a high flat-topped crown and wide curled brim, the forerunner of the top hat. The hair was still worn long occasionally, but unpowdered. Short hair, however, began to become popular. The cravat was replaced by a plain neckcloth.

THE WOMEN

Dress remained the same for women until about 1790, when new fashions began to appear from Revolutionary France. For the first thirty years of George III.'s reign the chief changes in fashion were the introduction of more and more ornamentation to gowns and under-skirts, the exaggeration of the size of the hoops worn, and elaboration in hairdressing and ornamentation. After about 1790 the hooped petticoat went out of fashion for day wear. The general form of the gown was the same, but the skirt hung straight and the waist line was slightly raised. The neck was still cut square and low, but the opening was filled by an enormous fichu, the ends of which were tucked into the neck in front, giving rather the appearance of a pouter pigeon. The hair was worn un-powdered with this type of dress.

By the beginning of the nineteenth century the Empire gown had come into fashion. This was a gown cut low in the neck and very high in the waist, with a long, straight skirt. For day use this dress was usually worn with long sleeves cut straight, in the evening a diminutive puff sleeve was usual. For ceremonial occasions the skirt was lengthened in a long, narrow train at the back. Bead embroidery was a popular form of ornamentation. Scarves of filmy material were fashionable. The hair was worn unpowdered, and turban head-dresses were usual among older women. Shoes were plain heel-less slippers fastened with ribbon round the ankle, like a child's dancing sandal.

THE LOWER CLASSES.—Up to the beginning of the nineteenth century there was no substantial change in the costume of the poorer people, except that the coats of the men became less and less full in the skirt. Country men still wore smocks. After the beginning of the nineteenth century the men began to use the cutaway coat and the women the Empire type of gown, but amongst the poorer people this was not cut so low in the neck nor was the waist so high. It was worn with a fichu, apron, and mob cap.

GEORGE IV

THE MEN

Costume remained substantially the same as it had been during the latter part of the preceding reign. The neckcloth was superseded by the stock, which was worn with a high stiff collar, the points of which reached up to just above the jaw-bone on each side of the face. The stock was similar to the neckcloth but shorter, and was made of thick black satin. Like the neckcloth, it was passed twice round the neck and tied in front in a knot, allowing the ends, which should be about 3 inches to 4 inches long after the knot is tied, to spread out sideways. The front of the shirt, which now showed, was stiffened by starch, and the opening down the front finished by a gathered frill. Breeches were still worn, but were sometimes replaced by trousers, which were made narrow in the leg

EMPIRE PERIOD DAY DRESS
From Ackermann's 'Repository of Arts'
The long sleeves are made from a contrasting material

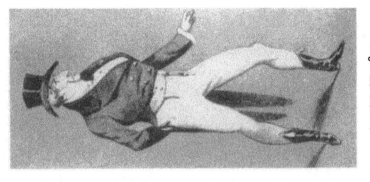
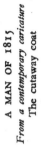

A MAN OF 1815
From a contemporary caricature
The cutaway coat

below the knee, and were fastened down to the instep by a strap passed under the shoe. Top hats became fashionable. The hair was worn short and was brushed forward at the temples.

THE WOMEN

Dress remained substantially the same. Towards the end of the reign, skirts began to get shorter for day wear, being about ankle length. Sleeves showed a tendency towards fullness. Caps of the turban type were worn by all married women indoors. Poke bonnets were worn.

THE LOWER CLASSES followed the trend of the richer people in fashion but were always rather later in adopting any change in dress. Breeches remained in use. Smocks were worn by country men.

WILLIAM IV

Costumes remained practically unchanged during this reign. Women's skirts continued to shorten until they reached about mid-calf. The skirts were made more full, and under them appeared the loose lace-edged legs of the pantalettes, which reached the ankle. Sleeves began to be cut in leg-of-mutton shape. Poke bonnets were used—and large muffs were very fashionable.

X. VICTORIAN COSTUME

FIRST PERIOD TO 1860

THE MEN

THE CUTAWAY COAT was replaced by the FROCK COAT, which had full straight skirts all round, and reached about three-quarter way down the thigh. This coat was invariably worn with trousers. The Top Hat became higher and straighter in the crown and narrower in the brim.

THE WOMEN

The skirt was no longer short enough to show the pantalettes, but was worn reaching to the ground. The tendency towards fullness developed rapidly until the crinoline petticoat came into fashion to distend the skirts. The gown was now frequently made in two parts—the bodice and skirt, the bodice being worn outside the skirt. Sleeves became plain or made three-quarter length and wide at the cuff, worn over an inner sleeve. The leg-of-mutton type was no longer fashionable. Bonnets were still worn, but they were no longer of the poke type, but small and close-fitting round the face. Caps which lay flat to the head and were trimmed with flowers, ribbon, and lace were worn in the house by married women. The hair was parted in the middle and drawn back into a knot at the nape of the neck, or was confined in a chenille net.

The Lower Classes showed the same trend of fashion, but the women distended the skirts with plain unwired petticoats.

SECOND PERIOD TO 1880

THE MEN

The Frock Coat went out of fashion except for ceremonial occasions. It was replaced by a short round jacket high in the revere. The frilled shirt front went out of fashion, and a plain shirt similar to the modern variety came in. Very little of it showed, as the waistcoat buttoned high in front to correspond with the high revere of the coat. A plain stiff collar, rather high, was worn and a narrow coloured tie. Trousers remained tight but were no longer strapped under the foot. Checked materials were extremely popular, and the coat and trousers were frequently made of different materials. Bowler hats with narrow curled brims in brown, grey, or black were popular,

W. P. FRITH: THE RAILWAY STATION

Holloway College, Windsor

Note the crinoline dress and close-fitting bonnet worn by the women and the frock-coat
and strapped trousers of the men

A BAR IN LONDON, MARCH 1886
From Max von Boehn's ' Modes and Manners of the XIXth Century

also straw 'boaters' and deer-stalker caps. The hair was worn cut short, and no longer was brushed forwards over the face at the temples. At this date man-tailoring is essential to obtain a good effect, and therefore no cutting diagram is given for the men's costume.

THE WOMEN

The crinoline gradually showed a backward trend until the hoops no longer went right round the skirt but were used only at the back to form a bustle. This developed an unevenness in the hem—the skirt being foot length in front but being extended to a very short train at the back. The bodice was frequently made with a fan-tailed lapel at the back which spread out over the bustle and accentuated it.

The bonnet went out of fashion and was replaced by a small round hat trimmed with flowers or feathers, and worn on the extreme top of the head, tilted forwards. Parasols with long handles were a fashionable adjunct to dress.

THE LOWER CLASSES showed the same trend, but the women did not use wire for extending the bustle but inserted a pad, usually of horse-hair, into a pocket concealed in the folds of the gown at the back.

GRAND NATIONAL ARCHERY MEETING
From Alan Bott's 'Our Fathers' (Heinemann)

DIAGRAMS

INTRODUCTORY NOTE.—These cutting diagrams are designed to allow 1-inch turnings on all seams. The sizes are stock sizes, and each pattern will therefore need its own adjustment to individual requirements ; it is advisable to tack the garment together and fit carefully to the wearer before finally making up.

SAXON MAN'S SHORT TUNIC

SCALE—⅛ in. to an inch.

SIZE OF PATTERN—Height, 5 ft. 8 in.; chest, 36 in. to 38 in.

MATERIAL REQUIRED—2½ yds. of material 48 in. wide.

METHOD—Stitch up side seams ABB; join sleeve at dotted line CB. Cut opening down front centre from neck to allow passage of head. Face back edges and pierce for lacing. Open left under-arm seam AB 4 in. or more at waist—face back, and fasten with hooks and eyes or press-fasteners. Allow 1 in. turnings on seams.

Note.—This pattern will also serve for the short tunic of the Norman Period. More care should be taken, however, during the later period to secure a close fit to the body from shoulder to hip, and also to make the sleeves fit the arm from elbow to wrist.

CODE—*w*, End of sleeve; face back or bind.

    x, Hem of garment.

    y, Fold of material.

    z, Avoid seam if possible.

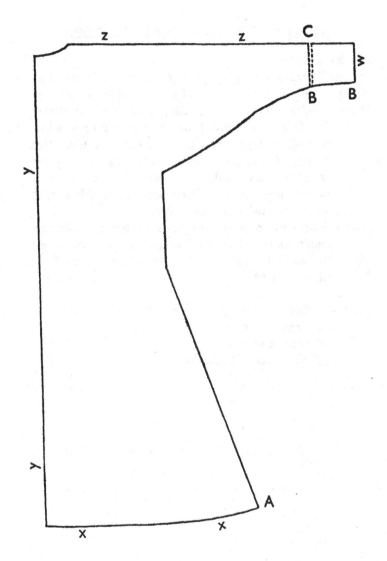

SAXON MAN'S LONG TUNIC OR ROBE

SCALE—⅛ in. to an inch.

SIZE OF PATTERN—Height, 5 ft. 8 in.; chest, 36 in. to 38 in.

MATERIAL REQUIRED—3½ yds. of material 48 in. wide.

METHOD—Stitch side seams ABB; join sleeve at dotted line BC. Cut opening down front centre to allow passage of head. Face back opening and pierce for lacing. Open left under-arm seam AB 4 in. or more at waist, face, and fasten with hooks and eyes or press-fasteners. Open sleeve seams BB 4 in. at wrist, face and fasten as above.

Note.—This pattern may also be used for the Norman man's robe. More care should be taken, however, to secure a close fit, especially in the sleeves from elbow to wrist.

CODE—*w*, End of sleeve; face back or bind.

    x, Hem of garment.

    y, Fold of material.

    z, Avoid seam if possible.

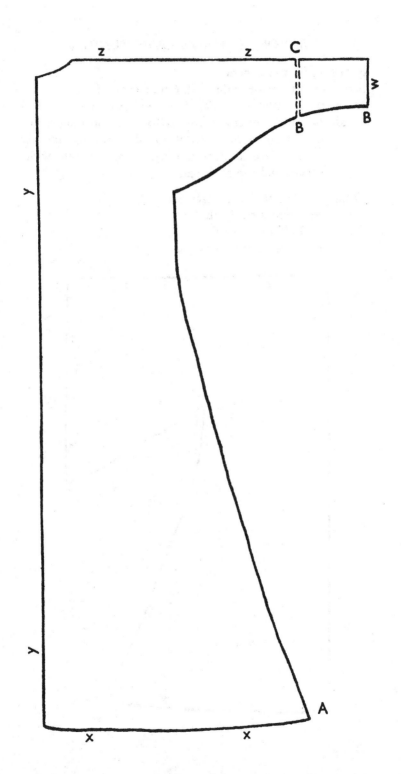

SAXON WOMAN'S OVER-TUNIC

SCALE—$\frac{1}{8}$ in. to an inch.

SIZE OF PATTERN—Height, 5 ft. 6 in. ; chest, 36 in.

MATERIAL REQUIRED—2 yds. of material 48 in. wide.

METHOD—Stitch up side seams ABB. Cut opening 6 in.
    deep from neck in front to allow for passage of
    head. Face back the opening and fasten with
    ornamental clip at throat.

CODE—*w*, End of sleeve ; face back.
    x, Hem of garment.
    y, Fold of material.
    z, Avoid seam if possible.

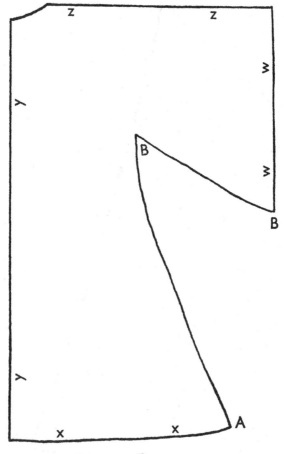

SAXON WOMAN'S COSTUME, SHOWING THE GOWN, OVER-TUNIC,
CIRCULAR CLOAK, AND HEAD-RAIL

(*Based on Harl. MS.* 2908. *British Museum*)

SAXON WOMAN'S GOWN

SCALE—$\frac{1}{8}$ in. to an inch.

SIZE OF PATTERN—Height, 5 ft. 6 in. ; chest, 36 in.

MATERIAL REQUIRED—$3\frac{1}{2}$ yds. of material 48 in. wide for robe with plain sleeve.

    $4\frac{1}{4}$ yds. of material 48 in. wide for robe with maunch sleeve.

METHOD—Stitch up side seams ABB ; join sleeve at dotted line BC. Cut an opening 6 in. deep from neck in centre front to allow passage of head. Face back right side of opening. Stitch left side between piece of doubled material to make over-lap for fasteners. Fasten with press-studs. In the case of the plain sleeve only, open sleeve seam BB 4 in. from wrist, face, and fasten with press-studs.

    Maunch Sleeve.—Stitch up under-arm seam BD ; join to gown at dotted line BC. Face back bag-opening DE.

Note.—This pattern can also be used for the Norman gown, but for later period a closer fit to the body should be secured by drawing in the side seams at the waist. In this case an opening in the left side seam is necessary—face back, and fasten with hooks and eyes. For the latest period, after the maunch sleeve ceased to be worn, the sleeve should be made tight-fitting from elbow to wrist. The seam should therefore be left open below the elbow and fastened with ornamental buttons.

CODE—*v*, End of maunch sleeve ; face back.

    w, End of narrow sleeve ; face back or bind.

    x, Hem of garment.

    y, Fold of material.

    z, Avoid seam if possible.

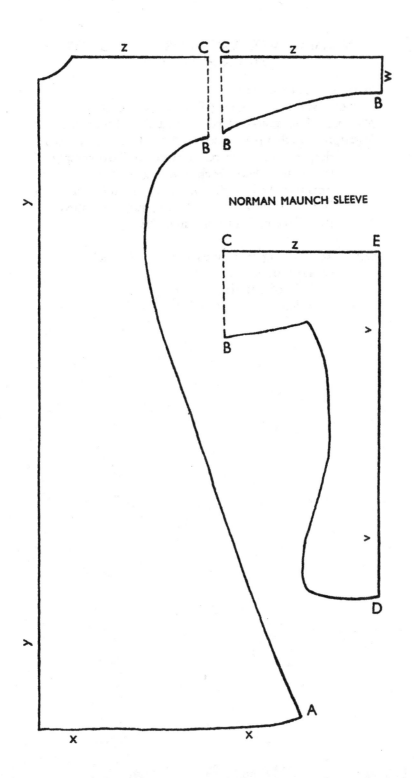

NORMAN MAUNCH SLEEVE

NORMAN WOMAN'S SHORT TUNIC WITH MAUNCH SLEEVE

SCALE—⅛ in. to an inch.

SIZE OF PATTERN—Height, 5 ft. 6 in.; chest, 36 in.

MATERIAL REQUIRED—3½ yds. of material 48 in. wide.

METHOD—Stitch up side seams AB. Cut opening 6 in. deep from neck in centre front to allow passage of the head. Face back opening and fasten with ornamental clip at throat. Stitch up under-arm seam BD of maunch sleeve. Join to tunic at dotted line BC. Face back bag-opening, DE.

CODE—*w*, Opening of maunch sleeve; face back.

x, Hem of garment.

y, Fold of material.

z, Avoid seam if possible.

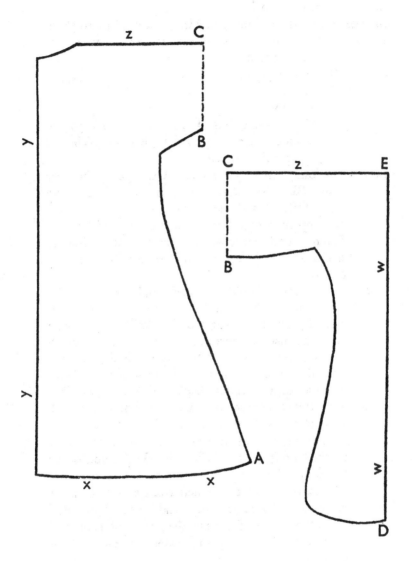

THE JUPON TUNIC

SCALE—$\frac{1}{8}$ in. to an inch.

SIZE OF PATTERN—Height, 5 ft. 8 in. ; chest, 36 in. to 38 in.

MATERIAL REQUIRED—3 yds. of material 48 in. wide.

    I. Back of tunic.

    II. Front of tunic.

    III. Sleeve.

    IV. Arm-band.

    V. Tippet.—Requires $\frac{3}{8}$ yd. of material 36 in. wide. Tippet may be plain or scalloped according to taste.

METHOD—Join under-arm seams AA. Join shoulder seams BB. Join dart CCC in sleeve. Join sleeve seam DD. Insert sleeve in armhole. Face back neck opening and hem. Join sleeve band EE and fasten round sleeve above elbow, placing join at sleeve seam. Join tippet FF to top of band, on outside.

Note.—This tunic should be very tight fitting. All seams should therefore be tacked, and the garment carefully fitted to wearer before finishing. It may either be made to button all up the front, in which case cut front panel in two pieces and face back opening, or to lace up the side, in which case leave left side seam open, face back, and pierce for lacing. The tippet should be made of white material. If desired, a skirt may be pleated on to the bottom of the tunic. This may be of a contrasting colour to the 'body part.' When the skirt is added, the fastening of the tunic should be under the arm. The skirt should be formed from a straight piece 72 in. long by 11 in. deep, and should be pleated on to the body of the tunic, the join being concealed by a belt. $\frac{3}{8}$ yd. of 36-in. material is required for the skirt.

CODE—*y*, Fold of material.

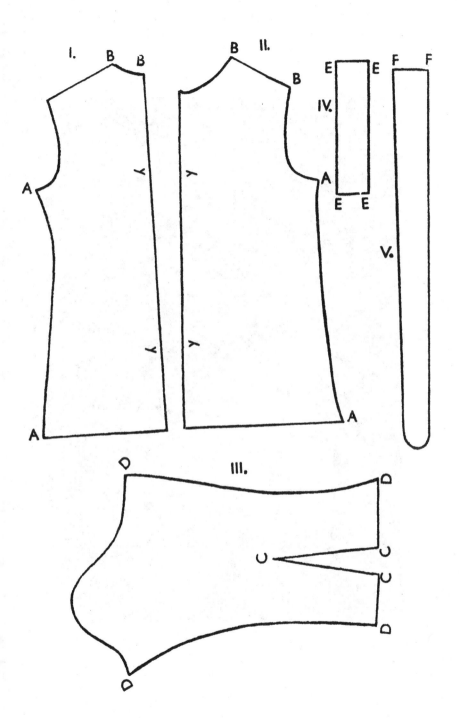

NORMAN WOMEN'S COSTUMES, SHOWING PENDENT SLEEVES

(Based on MS. Nero C. iv. British Museum)

THE COTE-HARDIE

(For Diagrams see following pages)

SCALE—⅛ in. to an inch.

SIZE OF PATTERN—Height, 5 ft. 6 in. ; chest, 36 in.

MATERIAL REQUIRED—5½ yds. of material 48 in. wide.

I. Front of bodice.
II. Back of bodice.
III. Sleeve.
IV. Centre section of skirt
V. Outside section of skirt.
VI. Cutting diagram for half circular skirt showing how material should be laid. Solid lines show seams. If possible, avoid seam at dotted line.

METHOD—Join bodice back and front at under-arm seams AA and shoulder seams BB, leaving left under-arm seam open 6 in. for fastening. Face back and fasten with hooks and eyes. Ditto left shoulder seam. Face back neck. Join dart CCC in sleeve. Join sleeve seams DD, leaving 6-in. cuff opening. Face back opening and cuff edge. Fasten opening with press-fasteners. Insert sleeve in armhole of bodice.

Join Section IV. and Section V. of skirt at EE. This forms half of the circular skirt. Join other half at FF, leaving 6 in. opening at left side. Face back and fasten with hooks and eyes. Join circular opening GG to bodice. (This circular opening will probably need adjustment to the bodice, care should be taken to obtain a smooth join without gathers.) Face back hem.

CODE—*y*, Fold of material.

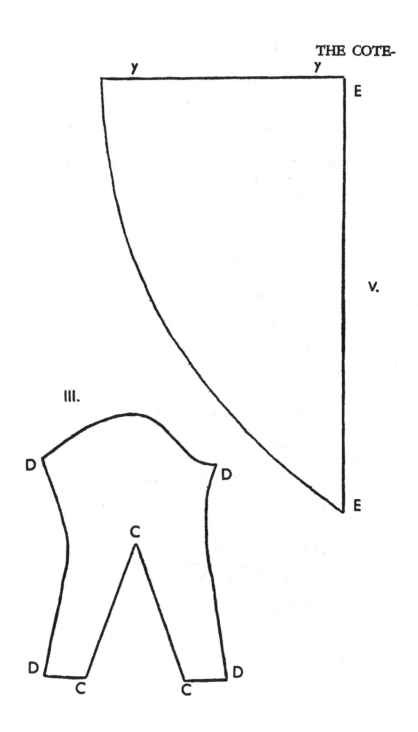

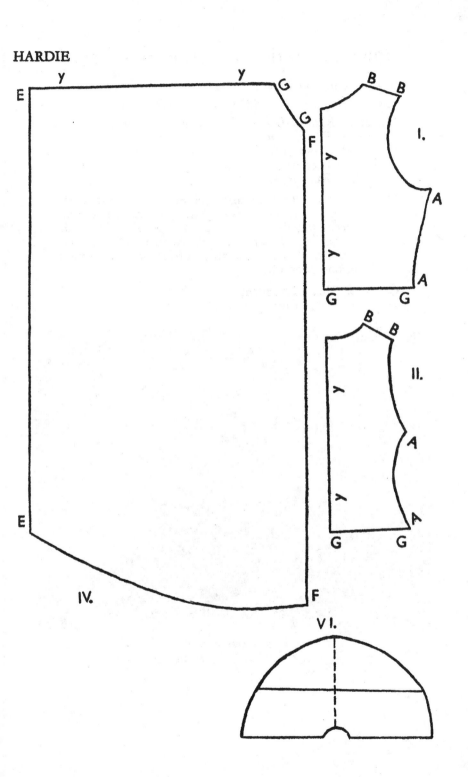

HARDIE

SIDELESS GOWN, WORN OVER COTE-HARDIE

SCALE—⅛ in. to an inch.

SIZE OF PATTERN—Height, 5 ft. 6 in.; chest, 36 in.

MATERIAL REQUIRED—5¼ yds. of material 48 in. wide.

    I. Front of gown.
    II. Front gore.
    III. Back of gown.
    IV. Back gore.

METHOD—Join gores to main pieces of back and front (Figs. 1 and 2) at seams AA. Join back and front pieces together at shoulder seams BB. Join side seams CC. Face back neck-opening and armholes. Trim with 4-in. wide strips of fur or velvet round armholes and hem.

CODE—*x*, Hem of garment.
     y, Fold of material.

SIDELESS GOWN
(*Harl. MS. 4425. British Museum*)

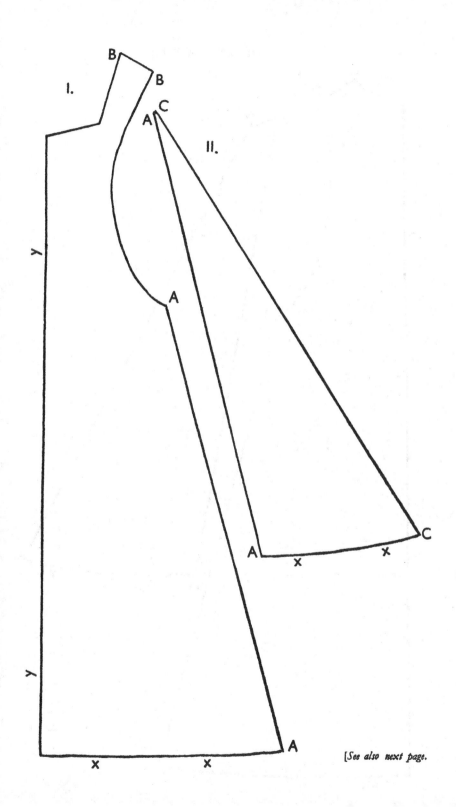

[See also next page.

SIDELESS GOWN

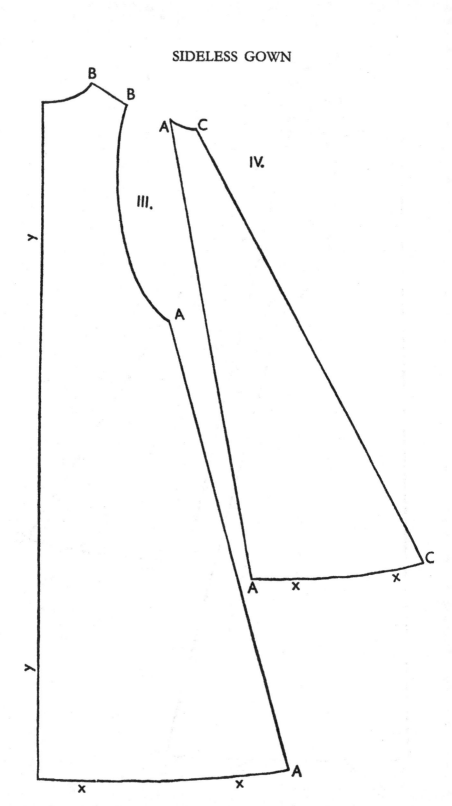

PLAIN SLEEVE AND HANGING SLEEVE

(For Diagrams see next page)

I. *Plain Sleeve.*

> SCALE—⅛ in. to an inch.
>
> MATERIAL REQUIRED—¾ yd. of material 48 in. wide.
>
> METHOD—Join dart BBB. Join arm seams AA. Insert sleeve in arm-hole, fitting point P to back of shoulder. Face back sleeve opening at wrist.

II., III., and IV. *Hanging Sleeve.*

> SCALE—⅛ in. to an inch.
>
> MATERIAL REQUIRED—2¼ yds. material 48 in. wide.
> 2¾ yds. of lining material.
>
> METHOD—Join back seam of upper sleeve AA. Cut lower sleeve, Section IV., together with lining material of contrasting shade and lighter weight. Join lining and sleeve at outer edge DD. Join upper and lower sleeve at CC. Sew down lining over join. Join front seam BB. Insert sleeve in armhole, fitting back seam AA halfway down back of armhole.

DAGGED SLEEVE

(For Diagram see page 85)

SCALE—⅛ in. to an inch.

MATERIAL REQUIRED—2¾ yds. of material 48 in. wide.
2¼ yds. of lining 48 in. wide.

METHOD—Turn in edges of daggings at serrated edge of sleeve and tack. Join up arm seams AA. Machine dagged edges. Insert sleeve into armhole, fitting point P to back of shoulder.

Note.—This sleeve should be lined with a plain material of contrasting colour, and the lining material should be of a lighter weight than that of the outside of the sleeve. Lining and sleeve should be cut together.

CODE—*y*, Fold of material.

PLAIN SLEEVE AND HANGING SLEEVE

DAGGED SLEEVE

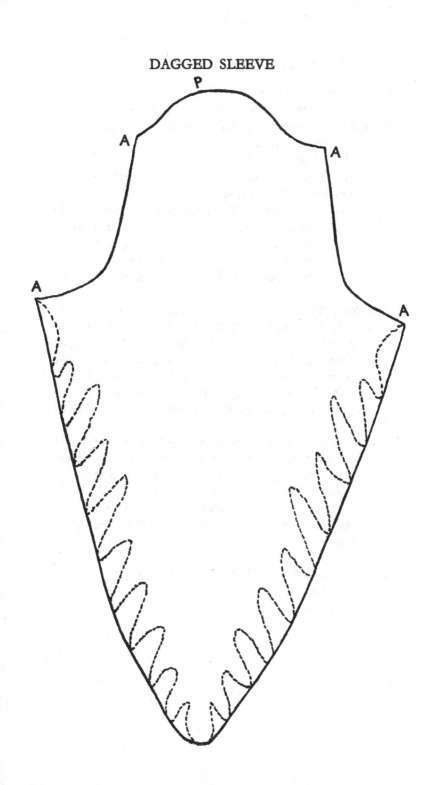

FOURTEENTH-CENTURY TUNIC

SCALE—⅛ in. to an inch.

SIZE OF PATTERN—Height, 5 ft. 8 in. ; chest, 36 in. to 38 in.

MATERIAL REQUIRED—2¾ yds. material 48 in. wide.

    I. Back of tunic.

    II. Front of tunic.

    III. Top of sleeve, made of lining material only.

    IV. Lower sleeve made from self material.

    V. Collar, cut in four sections, interlined with canvas, and lined with thinner material of contrasting colour to match lining of hanging or dagged sleeve. In event of plain sleeve being used, lining of collar should tone with tunic.

METHOD—Take in dart G in each side of waist of back. Join back and front at under-arm seams AA and shoulder seams BB. Join lower sleeve to upper sleeve lining at CC. Join sleeve seams DD. Insert sleeve in armhole, fitting point P to back of shoulder. Join collar sections EE. Join collar to neck-opening FF. Face back fronts HH and fasten with hooks and eyes.

Note.—The pattern for an inner sleeve given here is designed for use either with the hanging or dagged sleeves, diagrams for which are given on the preceding pages. With either of these sleeves, an inner sleeve is necessary. Should a plain sleeve be required, the pattern for same should be used without the inner sleeve.

CODE—w, End of sleeve ; face back or bind.

    x, Hem of garment.

    y, Fold of material.

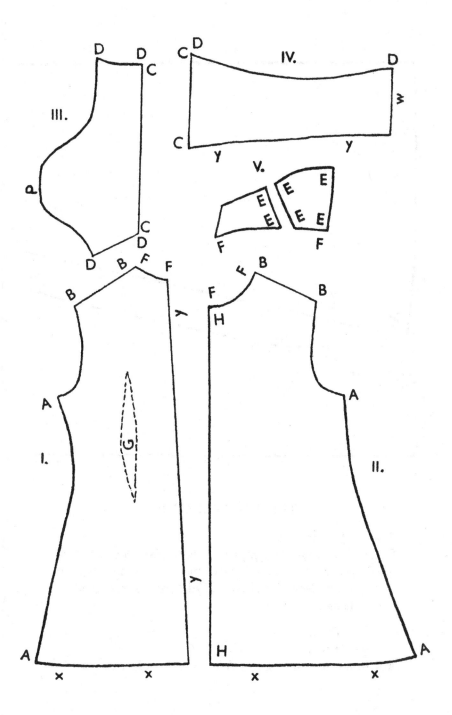

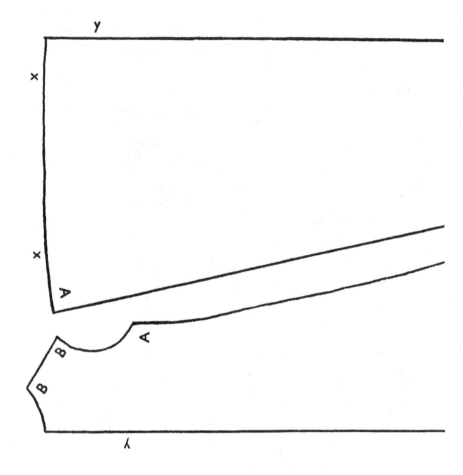

THE HOUPPELANDE

SCALE—$\frac{1}{8}$ in. to an inch.

SIZE OF PATTERN—Height, 5 ft. 8 in. ; chest, 36 in. to 38 in.

MATERIAL REQUIRED—4$\frac{1}{2}$ yds. material 48 in. wide if plain sleeve required. 2 yds. extra for dagged or hanging sleeves.

I. Front.
II. Back.

METHOD—Join side seams AA. Join shoulder seams BB.

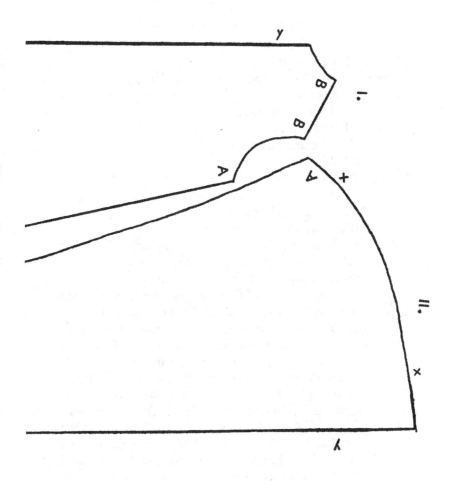

Any sleeve pattern given for Fourteenth-Century Tunic may be used. Collar may be as for tunic or a plain band 16 in. long and 2 in. deep. This should be lined with thin material and interlined with canvas. Cut opening 6 in. deep in centre front to allow passage of head. Face back and fasten with hooks and eyes.

CODE—*x*, Hem of garment.
       y, Fold of material.

HIGH-WAISTED GOWN

(For Diagrams see pages 92 and 93)

SCALE—⅛ in. to an inch.

SIZE OF PATTERN—Height, 5 ft. 6 in. ; chest, 36 in.

MATERIAL REQUIRED—4½ yds. of material 48 in. wide.

    I. Front of bodice.

    II. Back of bodice.

    III. V-shaped front vest.

    IV. Sleeve.

    V. Front panel of skirt.

    VI. Gore to front skirt panel.

    VII. Back panel of skirt.

    VIII. Gore to back skirt panel.

METHOD—Join dart AAA in front of bodice. Join dart BBB in back of bodice. Join side seams CC and shoulder seams DD. Face back neck-opening EE. Face back opening FF in back, and fasten with hooks and eyes. Insert vest (III.) into front opening, leaving left side free, and fastening with press-fasteners. Join dart GGG in sleve. Join seam HH, leaving opening 6 in. at cuff, face back and fasten with press-fasteners. Face back cuff. Insert sleeve in bodice, setting sleeve seam to point P in armhole. Join front gore (VI.) to front skirt panel (V.) at KK. Join back gore (VIII.) to back skirt panel at LL. Join front and back skirt panels from MM to end of each gore at bottom. Slit back panel at centre 6 in. from top to form placket, face back and fasten with press-studs. Pleat skirt into bodice at points J, otherwise sew in flat. Face back hem.

Note—Two front and two back gores are required, one for each side of each panel. This gown should be trimmed round hem, neck-opening, and sleeves with some contrasting material or with white fur. The join of bodice and skirt should be concealed by belt approximately 4 in. deep of contrasting material.

CODE—*y*, Fold of material.

HIGH-WAISTED GOWN: QUEEN ISABELLA AND HER LADIES OUT RIDING

From Froissart's 'Chronicles'

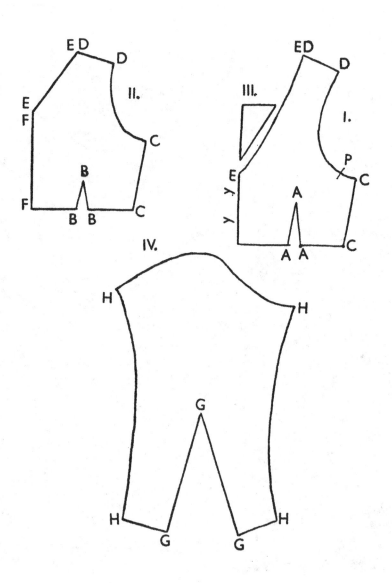

GOWN

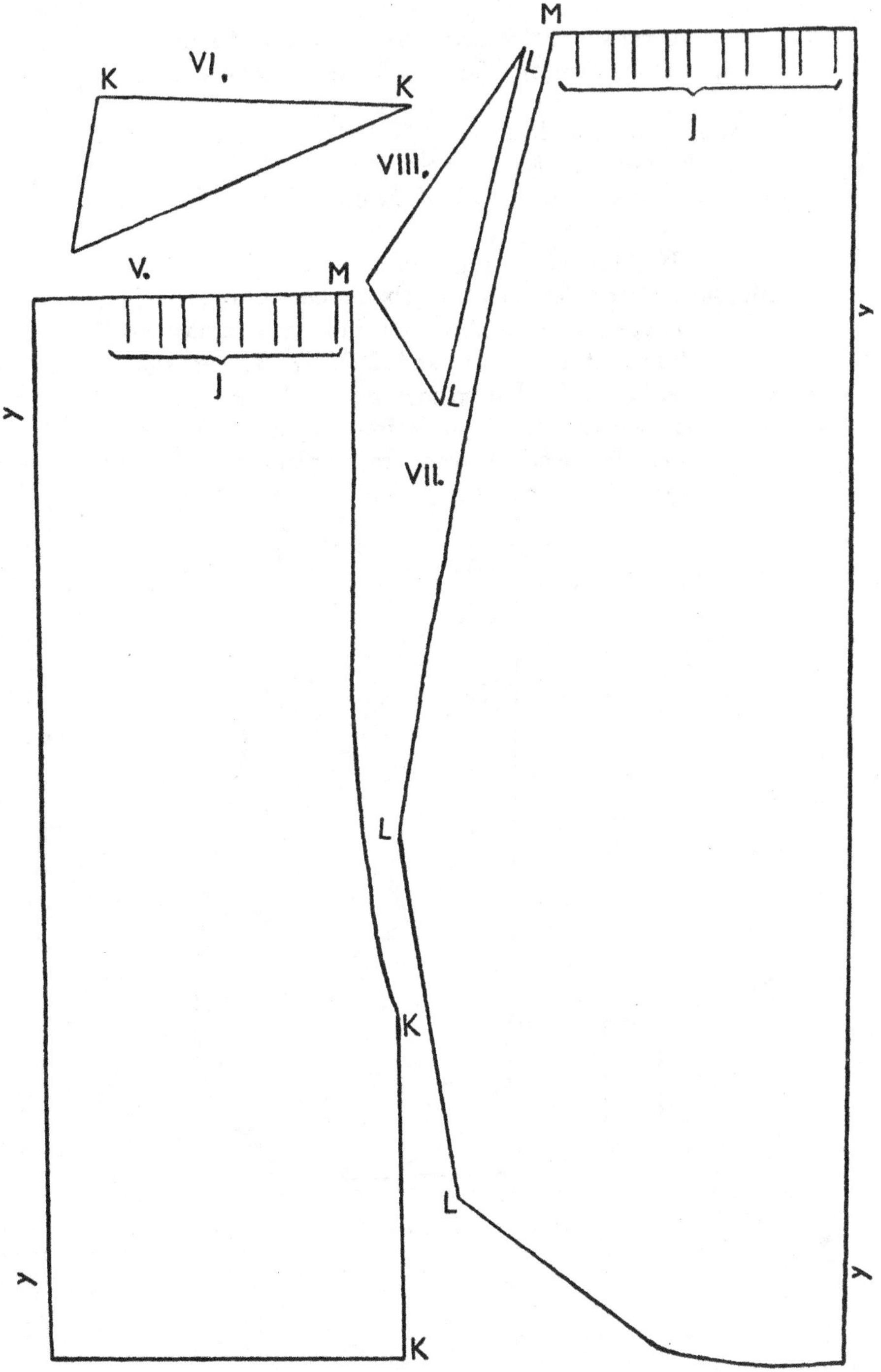

VI.

VIII.

V.

VII.

J

J

K K

M

L

L

M

L

K

L

K

Y Y Y Y

BAG SLEEVE

(ALTERNATIVE SLEEVE FOR HOUPPELANDE OR
MEDIEVAL TUNIC). Suitable for Edward IV period.

SCALE—⅛ in. to an inch.
SIZE—Height, 5 ft. 8 in. ; chest, 36 in. to 38 in.
MATERIAL REQUIRED—¾ yd. of material 48 in. wide.
    I. Sleeve.
    II. Cuff.
METHOD—Each sleeve and cuff should be cut double. Join
    outer-arm seam AA and inner-arm seam BBB.
    Join cuff seams CC and DD. Attach to sleeve.
    Gather EE and insert in armhole. When this sleeve
    is used for a tunic made from a patterned material
    it can be effectively made from a plain velvet to tone
    with one of the colours of the pattern.

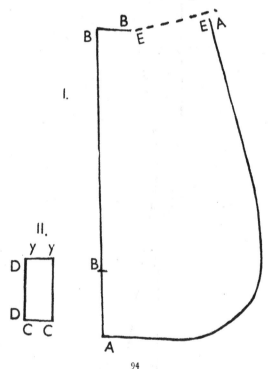

PETER OLIVER : SIR THOMAS MORE AND HIS FAMILY

Note the gable head-dress of the woman in front and the deep turn back to her outer sleeve

TUDOR SKIRTED DOUBLET AND TRUNKS

(*For Diagrams see pages 96 and 97*)

SCALE—$\frac{1}{8}$ in. to an inch.

SIZE OF PATTERN—Height, 5 ft. 8 in. ; chest, 36 in. to 38 in.

MATERIAL REQUIRED—$3\frac{3}{4}$ yds. material 48 in. wide for doublet; $\frac{3}{4}$ yd. white muslin to puff slashings. Trunks, $1\frac{1}{4}$ yd. material 48 in. wide.

  I. Front of doublet bodice.

 II. Back of doublet bodice.

IIIa. Puff of sleeve.

IIIb. Under - arm section of sleeve.

IIIc. Upper - arm section of sleeve.

IV. Collar band.

V. Skirt of doublet.

VI. Half-section of trunks.

Doublet.—

METHOD—The body of the doublet, neck-band and sleeve, sections 3b and 3c, should be interlined with canvas. Cut slashings S in front of doublet and in sleeve sections, puff slashings with muslin. Face back edges against canvas interlining, and edge outside with narrow braid. Join under-arm seams AA. Join shoulder seams BB. Join outer-arm seams DD and inner-arm seams CC, sections 3b, 3c. Join side seams of puff sleeves GG. Gather puff at EE and FF. Attach bottom of puff to sleeve at points HH. Tack top of puff to top of sleeve. Insert sleeve, with puff, into armhole, fitting point P to back of shoulder. Attach lining to neck-band and attach to doublet at JJ. Face back front opening, and fasten with hooks and eyes. Face back hem of doublet skirt. Pleat on doublet skirt to body at KK, using box pleats 2 to 4 in. wide according to stiffness of material.

     N.B.—*The diagram of doublet skirt allows for quarter width only. Two widths of material are necessary, with join at centre back.*

Trunks.—Half section of trunks. Cut from doubled material.

METHOD—Join leg seams AA together. Join back seam BB to back seam of second section. Join front seam CC to front seam of second section. Face back leg openings and top with wide tape. Thread elastic round legs and top.

Note.—Plain material should be used for trunks.

CODE—*w*, End of sleeve ; face back.

    x, Hem of garment.   *y*, Fold of material.

Note.—For Court costumes, wide braid may be used freely to strap doublet yoke and sleeves between slashings, and to hide join of yoke and skirt.

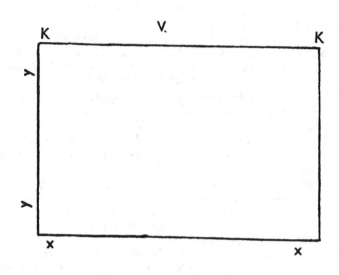

V.

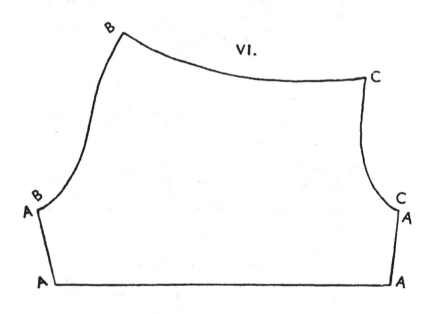

VI.

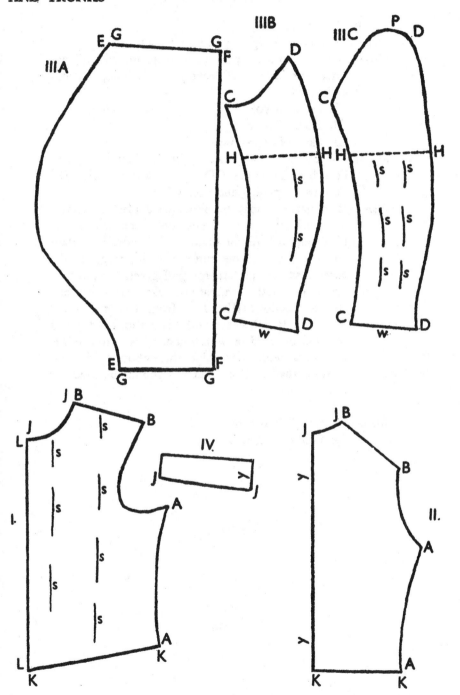

TUDOR OVER-GOWN

SCALE—⅛ in. to an inch.

SIZE OF PATTERN—Height, 5 ft. 6 in.; chest, 36 in.

MATERIAL REQUIRED—2 yds. material 48 in. wide (¾ yd. extra material for puff sleeves). 2 yds. lining material 48 in. wide.

    I. Front of yoke.

    II. Back of yoke.

    III. Skirt of over-gown.

METHOD—Join side seam AA. Join shoulder seams BB. Face back armholes DD. Join skirt to yoke EE. Face back opening and neck CC.

Note.—This garment may be either used plain as above, in which the front edges and neck should be bordered with fur or braid, or for more important characters it can have puff sleeves inserted. In the latter case, use pattern for puff given for doublet, lining the puff with pattern taken from doublet sleeves, sections III*b*, III*c*, from top to dotted line HH. Finish sleeve with plain 2 in. band of self material or band of wide braid. Trim front edges and neck with fur. Line throughout with contrasting shade. Plain material should be used for over-gown.

CODE—*x*, Hem of garment.

    y, Fold of material.

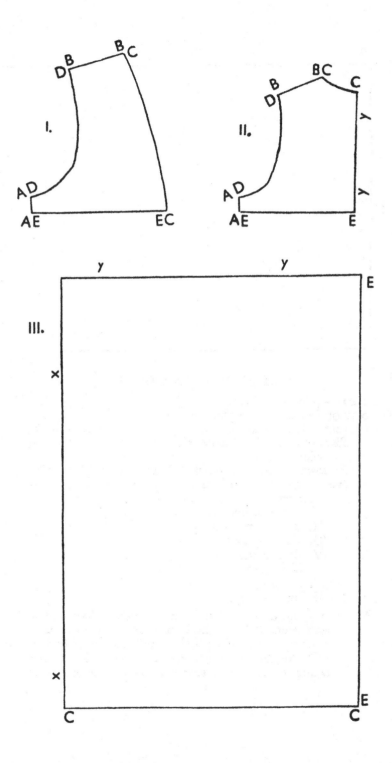

G   F

IV.

Λ

TUDOR WOMAN'S GOWN

SCALE—⅛ in. to an inch.

SIZE OF PATTERN—Height, 5 ft. 6 in. ; chest, 36 in.

MATERIAL REQUIRED—*Gown*, 6 yds. of material 48 in. wide.
    Sleeve facing 2 yds. of material 48 in. wide of contrasting colour.
    Petticoat, 2⅛ yds. of material 48 in. wide, preferably white.
    Inner sleeve, ½ yd. of material 48 in. wide, same as petticoat.

    I. Front of bodice.
    II. Back of bodice.
    III. Hanging sleeve.
    IV. Back panel of skirt.
    V. Side gore.
    VI. Front gore.
    VII. Inner sleeve.

METHOD—Join dart AAA in back of bodice. Join underarm seams BB and shoulder seams CC. Face back neck-opening. Face back front opening of bodice DD, and fasten with hooks and eyes. Cut sleeve facing for hanging sleeve as far as dotted line,

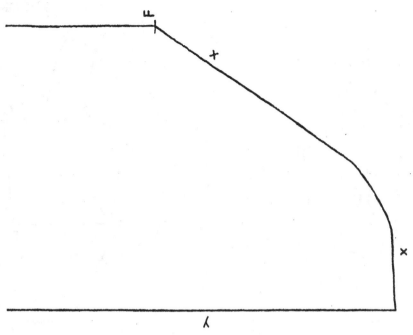

LL

+

x

ʎ

[Diagrams continued overleaf.

leaving upper arm unfaced. Stitch in facing.
Join sleeve seam EE. Insert sleeve in armhole. Join
side gore (V.) to back panel of skirt at FF. Join front
gore (VI.) leaving widest part at top at GG. Face
back front gore HH. Join skirt to bodice, pleating
fullness into back in 2-in. pleats. Leave centre front
of skirt open to show petticoat. Face back hem.

Cut petticoat in two panels, each 1¼ yds. long.
Join up selvedges at each side. Hem at bottom.
Face back top and run tape through. Join side
seams of inner sleeve JJ. Face back top of sleeve
KK and wrist LL, and run elastic through top and
bottom. Strap sleeve with six bands either of black
velvet ribbon 1 in. wide or bands of same material
as facing of hanging sleeve. Make strappings
slightly shorter than inner sleeve so that the sleeve
pouches slightly. Join each strap to the next with
a pearl at 4-in. intervals.

CODE—*x*, Hem of garment.
     y, Fold of material.

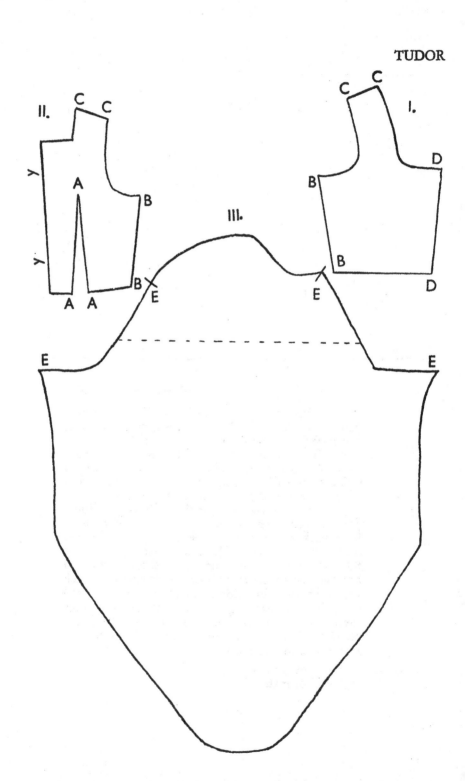

TUDOR

WOMAN'S GOWN

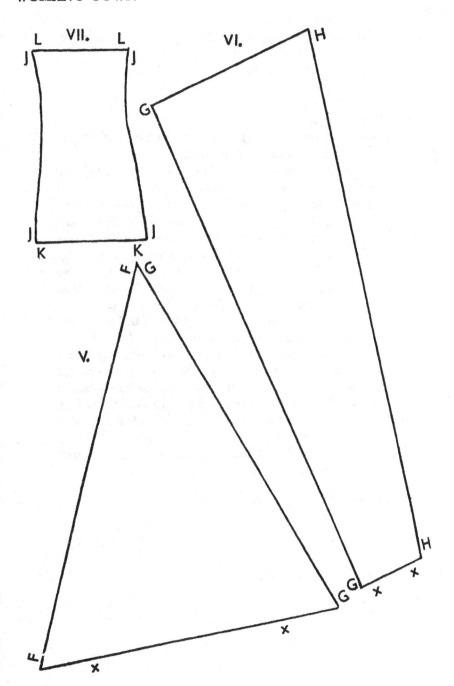

ELIZABETHAN DOUBLET

SCALE—$\frac{1}{8}$ in. to an inch.

SIZE OF PATTERN—Height, 5 ft. 8 in. ; chest, 36 in. to 38 in.
- I. Front of doublet.
- II. Back of doublet.
- III. Sleeve.
- IV. Basque.
- V. Collar band.

MATERIAL REQUIRED—Material for doublet and cape : 3¾ yds. of material 48 in. wide.

Material for trunks, cape lining, basque lining, and slash : 3½ yds. of material 48 in. wide.

METHOD—Join under-arm seams AA. Join shoulder seams BB. Cut slash in sleeve CC. Face back edges of slash and puff with loose fold of contrasting material. Form pleat at DD, stitching down edge towards outer seam of sleeve. Join outer sleeve seam EE. Join inner sleeve seam FF. Face back cuff opening. Insert sleeve in armhole, fitting top of seam EE to back of shoulder. Cut basque and basque lining on cross together. (The basque should be cut in two pieces, with opening centre front and centre back.) Face lining into basque at outer edge and sides. Join basque to doublet at GG. Face neck-band and join to doublet at HH. Face back doublet opening JJ, and fasten with hooks and eyes.

N.B.—This garment should be interlined with canvas throughout.

CODE—y, Fold of material.

t, Centre back.

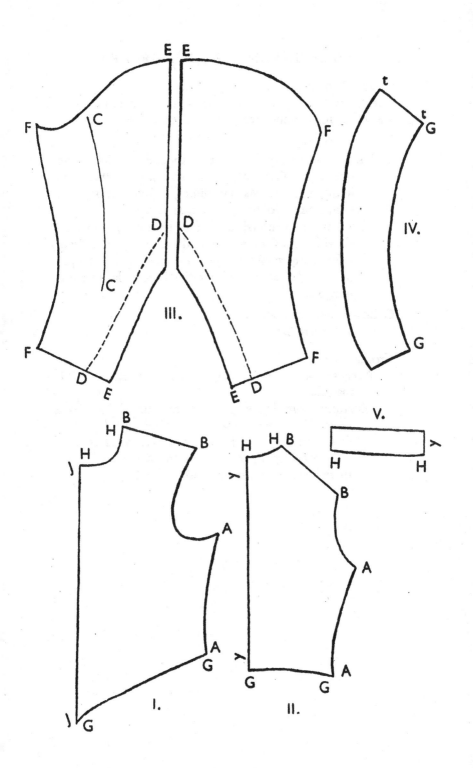

ELIZABETHAN CAPE AND TRUNKS

SCALE—⅛ in. to an inch.

SIZE OF PATTERN—5 ft. 8 in. ; chest, 36 in. to 38 in.

MATERIAL REQUIRED—See p. 104, Elizabethan Doublet.

Cape.—I. and II.

> METHOD—Cut cape and lining together. Face lining into cape. Cut collar in six sections together with lining and canvas interlining. Join sections at points BB. Join collar to cape at AA.
>
> *Note.*—If the material used for the cape is soft, an interlining of canvas should be used. The front lower corners of the cape may be either cut straight or rounded as shown by the dotted line of the diagram.
>
> CODE—*y*, Fold of material.
>
> *t*, Centre back.

Trunks.—III.

> PATTERN—Half section of trunks. Cut from double material.
>
> METHOD—Join leg seams AA together. Join back seam BB to back seam of second section. Join front seam CC to front seam of second section. Face back leg openings and top with wide tape ; thread elastic round legs and top.

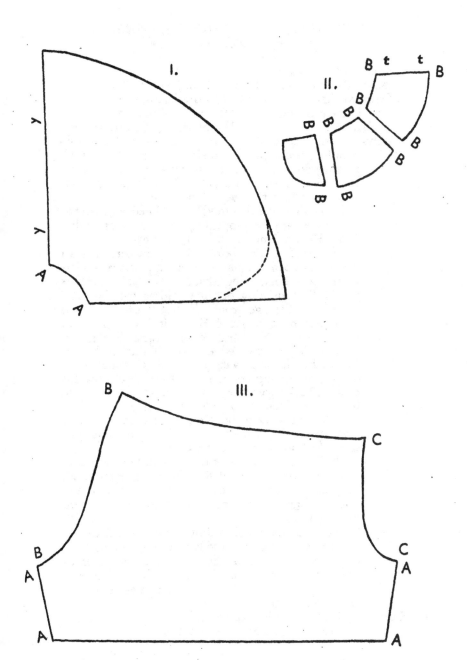

ELIZABETHAN WOMAN'S BELL-SHAPED DRESS

SCALE—$\frac{1}{8}$ in. to an inch.

SIZE OF PATTERN—Height, 5 ft. 6 in. ; chest, 36 in.

MATERIAL REQUIRED—5 yds. of material 48 in. wide.

I. Back of bodice.   II. Front of bodice.

III. Sleeve.   IV. Skirt.   V. Stomacher.

METHOD—Join darts CCC. Join side seams AA. Join shoulder seams BB. Pleat sleeve at dotted lines GG, tacking down pleat edge towards seam EE. Gather top of sleeve between points FF. Join sleeve seams DD-EE. Insert sleeve into armhole.

N.B.—The sleeve should be interlined with canvas.

Face back neck-opening and fronts of bodice KK. Fasten fronts with hooks and eyes.

Section IV. The Skirt.—The Elizabethan skirt was worn open in front, showing a petticoat underneath in a contrasting shade. The skirt itself is very full, consisting of three widths cut the same except for the two front edges at the top. Shape these down at points HH to fit lower point of bodice front. Fold back along dotted line LL to make facing to skirt edge. Attach skirt to bodice JJ, setting in skirt with heavy pleats about 3 in. deep, overlapping about 1 in. Face pleats towards back. Tack stomacher over canvas lining. Run bone down centre to point M. Line stomacher. Attach stomacher to bodice so that point M meets lower point M of bodice. Stitch down right side, attach left side with press-fasteners.

N.B.—Dress as above to be worn over petticoat and BELL farthingale. If RING farthingale required, lengthen pattern of bodice 1 in. all round and extend point of stomacher 1 in. Shorten skirt 1 in. Add waist ruff.

To make waist ruff.—Allow $\frac{1}{2}$ yd. extra material. Cut into two strips 9 in. wide and join, making long strip 9 in. wide. Fold down middle and press to reduce width to $4\frac{1}{2}$ in. Set into waist in 5-in. box pleats. For description of farthingales, see Historical Notes, p. 47.

CODE—*w*, End of sleeve ; face back.

x, Hem of garment.   *y*, Fold of material.

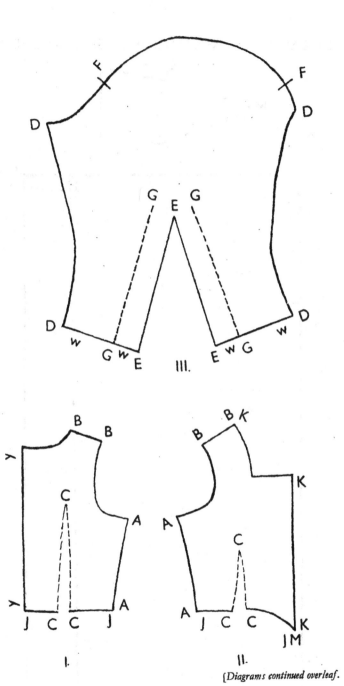

III.

I.

II.

[Diagrams continued overleaf.

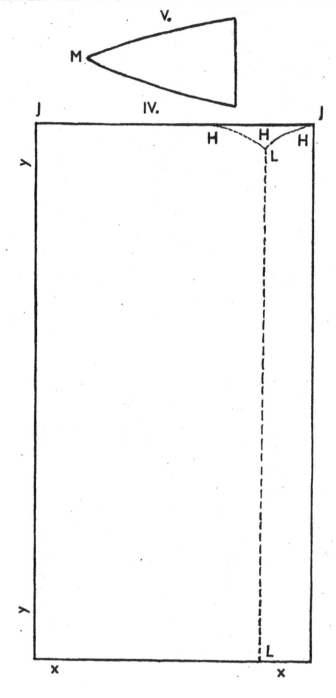

PROCESSION OF QUEEN ELIZABETH TO THE MARRIAGE OF LORD HERBERT AND MISS ANNE RUSSELL AT
BLACKFRIARS, JUNE 16, 1600

CHARLES I MAN'S DOUBLET

SCALE—⅛ in. to an inch.

SIZE—Height, 5 ft. 8 in. ; chest, 36 in. to 38 in.

MATERIAL REQUIRED—*Doublet*, 2¼ yds. of material 48 in. wide.

Inner sleeves and collar, 1¼ yds. lawn 48 in. wide ; 2 yds. point lace for edging.

I. Front of doublet. (Cut double.)
II. Back of doublet.
III. Front tab. (Cut double.)
IV. Side tab. (Cut double.)
V. Back tab. (Cut double.)
VI. Sleeve.
VII. Epaulette. (Cut double.)
VIII. Collar.

METHOD—Join under-arm seams AA. Join shoulder seams BB. Face back fronts and fasten with hooks and eyes. Interline all six tabs with canvas, and face. (Sufficient scraps of material should be left over after cutting to allow for this.) Join tabs to waist of doublet. Slash sleeve SS, and face back. Pleat over edges of dart CC. Join dart DDD. Join sleeve seam EE. Insert sleeve in armhole. Line epaulette (VII.) with canvas. Join edges FF. Stitch straight-folded edge of epaulette to top of armhole. Join seam GG of inner sleeve (see page 115). Make ½ in. deep hem top and bottom. Edge wrist with lace HH. Run elastic through hems. Add collarband 1 in. deep to collar at JJ. Roll outer edge of collar and finish with lace. Trimming may be used in the form of small ornamental buttons down right front of doublet, and braid round waist and along edges of sleeve slash and epaulette.

CODE—*y*, Fold of material.

t, Centre back.

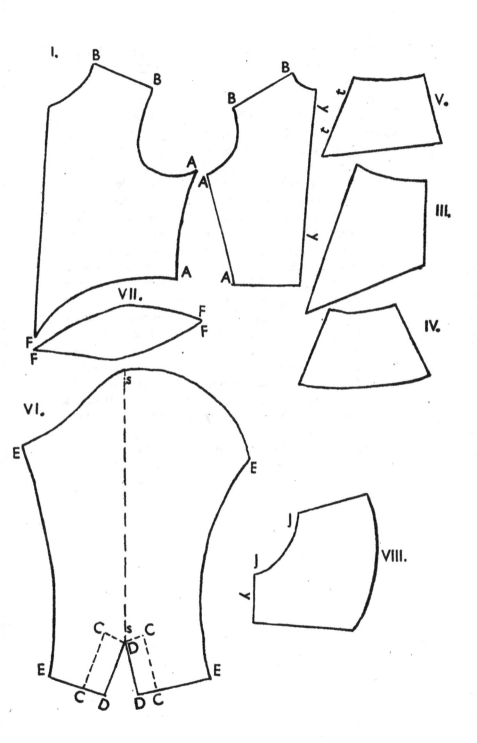

CHARLES I INNER SLEEVE AND CHARLES I AND CHARLES II BREECHES

SCALE—⅛ in. to an inch.

SIZE—Height, 5 ft. 8 in. Chest, 36 in. to 38 in.

MATERIAL REQUIRED—2 yds. of material 48 in. wide;
2 yds. of lining material 48 in. wide.

IX. Inner sleeve (Charles I).

X. Front panel of breeches. (Cut double.)

XI. Back panel of breeches. (Cut double.)

METHOD—Join darts PP in back and front pieces. Join seams AA of back and front pieces to form leg. Join two front pieces at BB, join two back pieces at CC. Join sides DD. Face back EE in sides front. Stitch flaps to sides back FF. Fasten these openings with hooks and eyes. Add braces buttons. Cut lining similar to breeches, but make legs 2 in. shorter. Make up lining separately. Stitch in lining at top of breeches, crutch, and knees. This will give a pouched effect to the knees of the breeches. The side seams of the breeches may be ornamented with braid, and for Charles II men a knot of bright ribbon may be added at the outside of each knee.

Note.—For directions for making up inner sleeve, see note on Charles I Doublet.

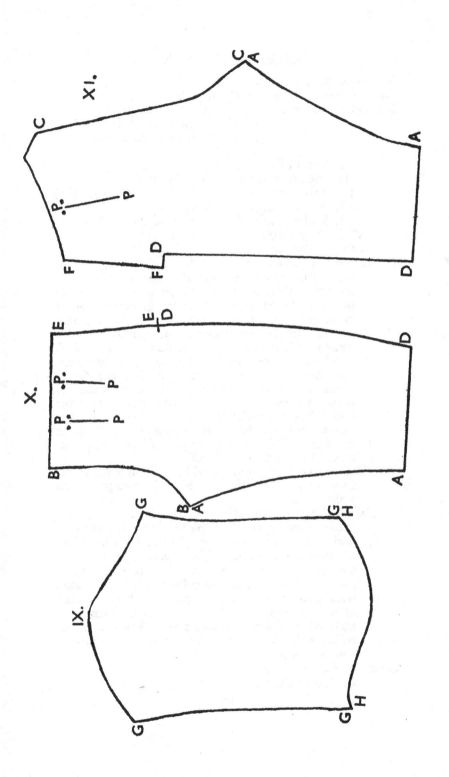

CHARLES I LADY'S GOWN

SCALE—$\frac{1}{8}$ in. to an inch.

SIZE—Height, 5 ft. 6 in. ; chest, 36 in.

MATERIAL REQUIRED—5 yds. material 48 in. wide.

      $1\frac{1}{2}$ yds. lining 36 in. wide.

      $\frac{3}{4}$ yds. organdie 48 in. wide.

      5 yds. point lace.

   I. Front of bodice. (Cut double.)

   II. Back of bodice.   III. Stomacher.

   IV. Tabs for waist.   V. Sleeve. (Cut double.)

   VI. Sleeve lining. (Cut double.)

   VII. Under collar. (Cut on the cross.)

   VIII. Over collar. (Cut on the cross.)

   IX. Collar band.

METHOD—Join under-arm seams AA and shoulder seams BB. Run gathering-threads through top and bottom of sleeve. Join sleeve seam CC. Join seam of sleeve lining DD. Draw up gathering-threads of sleeve until it fits lining. Stitch lining into sleeve. Insert lined sleeve into armhole. Face waist tabs (Section IV.). Join waist tabs to bodice. Stitch bone down centre of stomacher, then face. Face back neck and fronts of bodice, and fasten fronts with hooks and eyes. Attach stomacher to bodice so that point is level with bottom of waist tabs. Sew stomacher down on right side bodice. Leave open on left side and fasten with press fasteners. Finish sleeve with cuff of lace with points tacked back over sleeve puff.

Skirt.—Make skirt from $2\frac{1}{4}$ widths of the material cut 42 in. long. Hem bottom. Pleat top into petersham waist-band.

Collar.—This is made of two collar pieces, the smaller laid over the larger. Each piece is separate and edged with lace all round, except when both are joined to the same collar band. Whip outer edges of under and over collars and attach collars to collar band. Edge both under and over collars with lace. Fasten collar band with hook and eye. Attach centre back of collar to centre back of bodice neck. Tack in on each side as far as shoulder seam. The join of the collar in front may be trimmed by loose bow of narrow ribbon.

CODE—*y*, Fold of material.

   w, Top of sleeve.

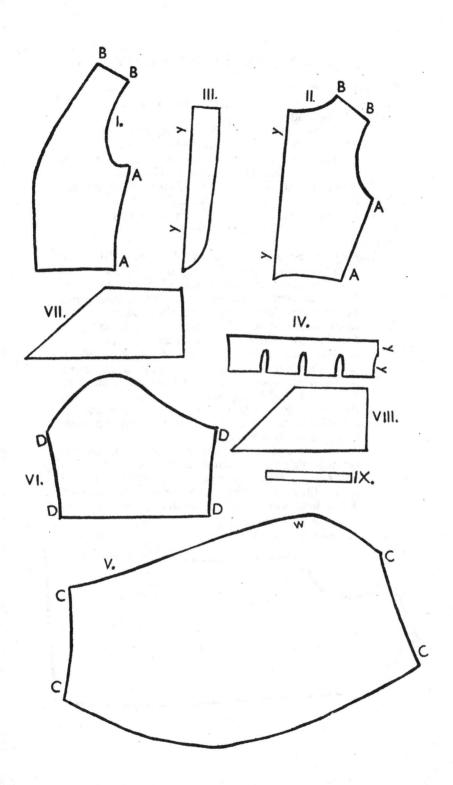

CHARLES II MAN'S COAT AND VEST

SCALE—$\frac{1}{8}$ in. to an inch.

SIZE—Height, 5 ft. 8 in. ; chest, 36 in. to 38 in.

MATERIAL REQUIRED—

    Coat—2½ yds. material 48 in. wide, ditto lining.

    Vest—1 yd. material 48 in. wide, ditto lining.

    Breeches—2 yds. material 48 in. wide (use same pattern as for Charles I Gentleman).

I. Front of coat.	IV. Under half of sleeve.
II. Back of coat.	V. Cuff.
III. Top of sleeve.	VI. Front of vest.

(All cut double.)

METHOD—

    Coat—Join dart AAA. Join shoulder seam BB. Join under-arm seam CC, leaving open below dotted line. Repeat with other side of coat. Join two halves of coat at centre seam DD, leaving open below dotted line. Join outer sleeve seam EE and inner sleeve seam FF. Insert sleeve in armhole. Interline cuff with canvas. Line and attach to sleeve at GG. Cut pocket slot HH and face back edges. Line coat throughout. Trim with braid down fronts, down open edges of each seam in coat skirt, round cuff, and along each side of pocket opening. Add shoulder-knots of ribbon at sleeve end of shoulder-seam BB so that ribbon hangs approximately 4 in. over sleeve.

    Vest—Use same pattern for vest back as for Eighteenth-century Waistcoat. Join shoulder seams and under-arm seams. Line fronts and fasten with hooks and eyes. Ornament with small ornamental buttons down left front. Attach adjustable strap to side seams at each side.

CODE—*y*, Fold of material.

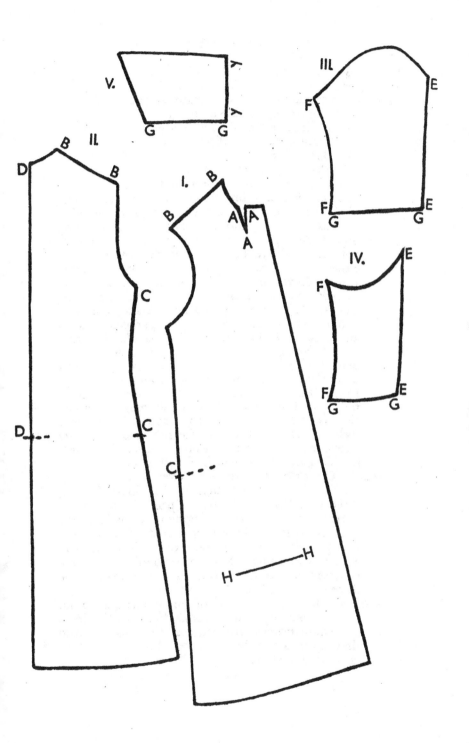

CHARLES II LADY'S GOWN

SCALE—⅛ in. to an inch.

SIZE—Height, 5 ft. 6 in. ; chest, 36 in.

MATERIAL REQUIRED—6¼ yds. of material 48 in. wide.

    ¾ yds. organdie for sleeve lining.

    3½ yds. lining material 36 in. wide.

    I. Front of bodice. (Cut double.)

    II. Back of bodice.

    III. Sleeve. (Cut double.)

METHOD—Join darts AAA in back and front of bodice. Join under-arm seam BB and shoulder seam CC. Slash sleeve SS and face back. Run two gathering threads one along top of sleeve and second along dotted line DD. Join sleeve seam EE. Face back bottom of sleeve FFFF. Join slash at points P either with large pearl or small knot of ribbon. Insert sleeve in armhole, pulling up gathering threads until sleeve top is the right size, and taking care to disperse gathers evenly. Using the same pattern, cut inner sleeve from organdie, allowing an extra 2 in. in length. Run single gathering thread through top of sleeve. Join seam. Make hem ¼ in. deep at bottom of sleeve and insert inner sleeve in armhole, having drawn up gatherings to fit. Run elastic through hem of sleeve to form puff. Pull organdie through slashing of upper sleeve. When wearing, push elastic of inner sleeve well up arm, so that only the pouch of the inner sleeve shows below hem of outer sleeve. If desired, the inner sleeve may be edged with lace.

    Skirt—The skirt is worn open over a petticoat. It requires three widths of material 42 in. long. Join the three strips leaving the front open. Hem bottom. Pleat top on to bodice, arranging pleats as far to the back as possible. Face back fronts. Sew a string of tape 9 in. long at a point 24 in. from waist at each side opening. Sew corresponding tape at a point 15 in. from waist in each side seam. Tie these on each side to loop skirt.

    Petticoat—Join three widths of lining material 42 in. long. Hem top and bottom. Face on the front one width material for petticoat front panel. Run draw-string along the top.

CODE—*y*, Fold of material.

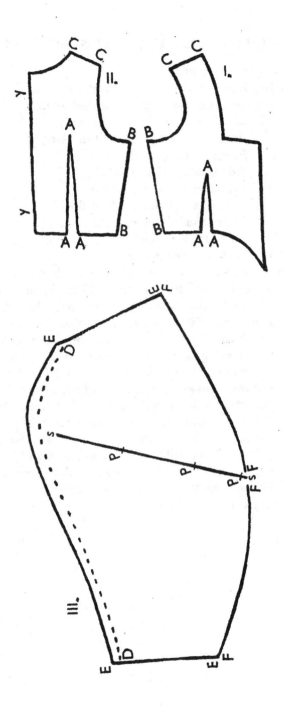

SCALE—⅛ in. to an inch.

SIZE—Height, 5 ft. 8 in. ; chest, 36 in. to 38 in.

MATERIAL REQUIRED—3½ yds. of material 48 in. wide.

    3½ yds. of lining material 48 in. wide.

    I. Front panel of coat. (Cut double.)

    II. Front gore. (Cut double.)

    III. Side panel. (Cut double.)

    IV. Back panel. (Cut double.)

    V. Under half of sleeve. (Cut double.)

    VI. Upper half of sleeve. (Cut double.)

    VII. Cuff. (Cut double.)

    VIII. Pocket. (Cut double.)

METHOD—Join gore to front panel AA. Join side panel to back panel BB and CC. Form inverted pleat DD with fold in line with seam BB. Join under-arm seam EE. Repeat with other half of coat. Join two halves at centre back FF. Face back flap GG, leaving skirt open at centre back. Join outer sleeve seam HH and inner sleeve seam JJ. Interline cuff with canvas. Join lining and outer cuff at KKK. Join cuff to sleeve end LL and double back. Insert sleeve in armhole. Interline pocket flap with canvas, face and attach to coat at MM. Stitch in lining. Trim with braid round cuff and pocket edges and down front edges. Add ornamental buttons down right front, and one on each pleat end at back of waist.

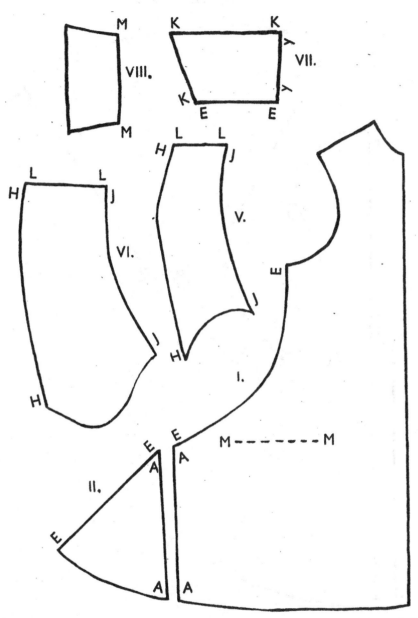

[*Diagrams continued overleaf.*

FULL-SKIRTED COAT

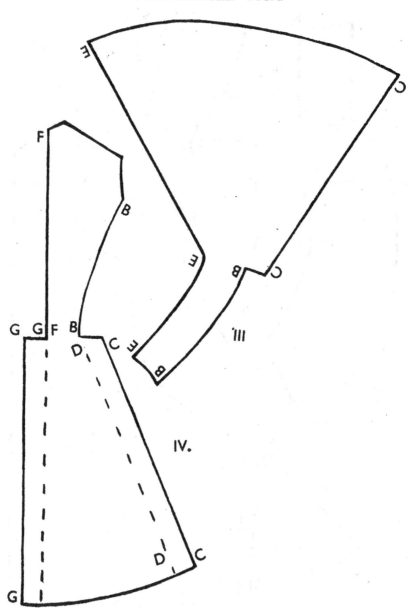

THE STAGE IN THE EIGHTEENTH CENTURY

From an engraving of Hogarth's picture, 'The Beggar's Opera,' by William Blake

Note the George I full-skirted coat

EIGHTEENTH-CENTURY FULL-SKIRTED WAISTCOAT

SCALE—⅛ in. to an inch.

SIZE OF PATTERN—Height, 5 ft. 8 in. ; chest, 36 in. to 38 in.

MATERIAL REQUIRED—1 yd. of material 48 in. wide. ¾ yd. of lining material 48 in. wide.

METHOD—Cut fronts of waistcoat and front linings together. Face linings into fronts along hem, front openings, neck and armholes.   Join front of waistcoat to back at under-arm seam AA and shoulder seam BB.   Bind neck and hem of back of waistcoat. Stitch down lining to under-arm shoulder seams.   Fasten fronts with hooks and eyes.   Ornament, if desired, with braid down the edges of the fronts and along the hem or with small ornamental buttons down right front. Attach adjustable strap at point P in under-arm seam.

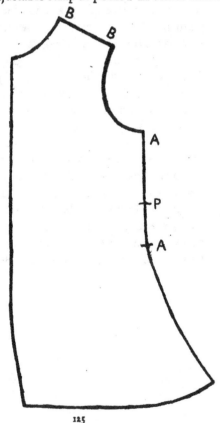

EIGHTEENTH-CENTURY SQUARE-CUT COAT

SCALE—⅛ in. to an inch.

SIZE OF PATTERN—Height, 5 ft. 8 in. ; chest, 36 in. to 38 in.

MATERIAL REQUIRED—3 yds. of material 48 in. wide.
Ditto of lining material.
    I. Front panel of coat. (Cut double.)
    II. Back panel of coat. (Cut double.)
    III. Upper sleeve. (Cut double.)
    IV. Under sleeve. (Cut double.)
    V. Cuff. (Cut double.)
    VI. Pocket flap. (Cut double.)

METHOD—Join under-arm seam AA, and side seam of
coat skirt BB. Make inverted pleat at side seam BB
so that edges of pleat are in line with under-arm
seam AA. Join centre back seams CC. Fold back
skirt at DD, so that edges of pleat are in line
with centre back seam CC. Join shoulder seams.
Tack back front edges of coat. Join inner sleeve
seam FF and outer sleeve seam GG. Interline
cuff with canvas and join at HH. Attach cuff
to sleeve at JJ. Insert sleeve in armhole. Interline pocket flap with canvas and attach at KK.
Line coat throughout. Trim with ornamental
buttons down right front and at each point of
pocket flap, allowing three buttons for each pocket.
If desired, braid may be used to trim left front of
coat, making indentations as if edging buttonholes, and also may be used to edge cuffs and pocket
flaps. This coat is not meant to do up.

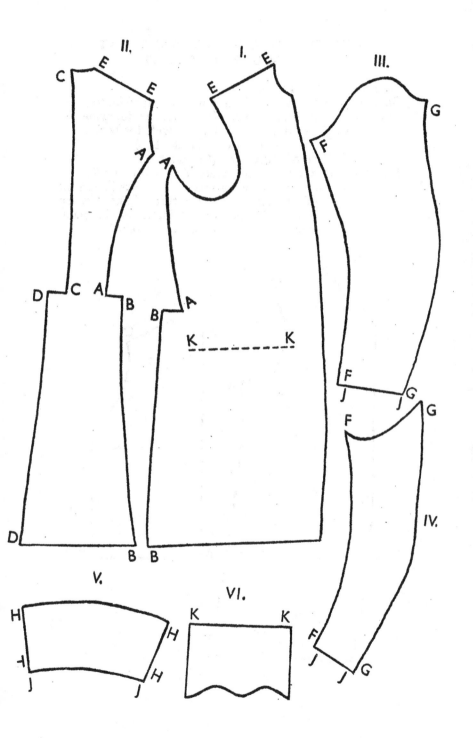

EIGHTEENTH-CENTURY WAISTCOAT
FOR SQUARE-CUT COAT

SCALE—$\frac{1}{8}$ in. to an inch.

SIZE OF PATTERN—Height, 5 ft. 8 in. ; chest, 36 in. to 38 in.

MATERIAL REQUIRED—1 yd. of material 48 in. wide for
fronts. 1 yd. of material 48 in. wide for back.

    I. Front of waistcoat. (Cut double.)
    II. Back of waistcoat. (Cut double.)

METHOD—Join centre back seam AA. Join under-arm
seam BB. Join shoulder seams CC. Tack back front
edges of waistcoat and line throughout. Fasten
fronts with hooks and eyes. Trim fronts with braid.
Attach strap to back of waistcoat at point P.

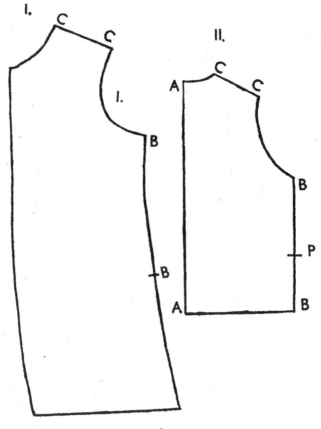

EIGHTEENTH AND NINETEENTH-CENTURY BREECHES

SCALE—⅛ in. to an inch.
SIZE—Height, 5 ft. 8 in.; chest, 36 in. to 38 in.
MATERIAL REQUIRED—2 yds. of material 48 in. wide.
      I. Front panel of breeches. (Cut double.)
     II. Back panel of breeches. (Cut double.)
METHOD—Join seam AA of front and back pieces to form
    leg; join two front pieces at BB and join two back
    pieces at CC. Join sides DD. Face back side
    fronts EE and FF. Stitch flaps to sides back GG, HH.
    Fasten these openings with hooks and eyes. Face
    back knees and top of breeches. Add brace buttons.

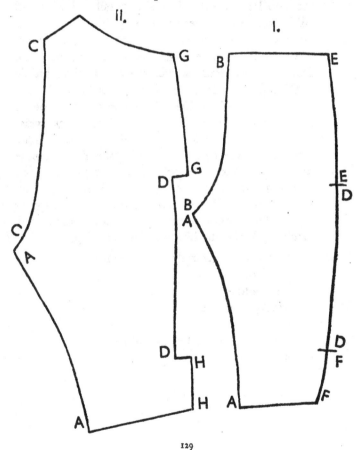

EIGHTEENTH-CENTURY PANNIER PETTICOAT

SCALE—⅛ in. to an inch.

SIZE—Height, 5 ft. 6 in.; chest, 36 in.

MATERIAL REQUIRED—3 yds. material 48 in. wide; 2 yds. crinoline wire. Tape.

    I. Centre front panel of skirt. (Cut double—for back ditto.)

    II. Saddle. (Cut double.)

    III. Side panel of skirt. (Cut double.)

    IV. Diagram of completed garment.

METHOD—Join front panel (Section I.) to side panel (Section III.) at AA. Join side panel to back panel BB. Join back panel to second side panel in the same way. Join second side panel to front panel at CC. Gather side panels along dotted line DD. Draw up and attach gathered side panel to saddle at EEE. Attach front and back panels to saddle FF. Repeat with other side. Sew continuous tape to take crinoline wire along GG. Face back waist of petticoat HH with tape, and run draw-thread through. Face back hem with tape for crinoline wire. Run wire through tapes at hips and hem, allowing a slightly greater circumference at hem. At the points KK on each saddle attach strips of tape. These should be tied together sufficiently firmly to flatten the hip wire into an ellipse.

DIAGRAM IV. shows the completed garment :

    I. Front panel.

    II. Saddle.

    III. Side panel.

CODE—w, Hip wire flattened to an ellipse.

    z, Hem wire.

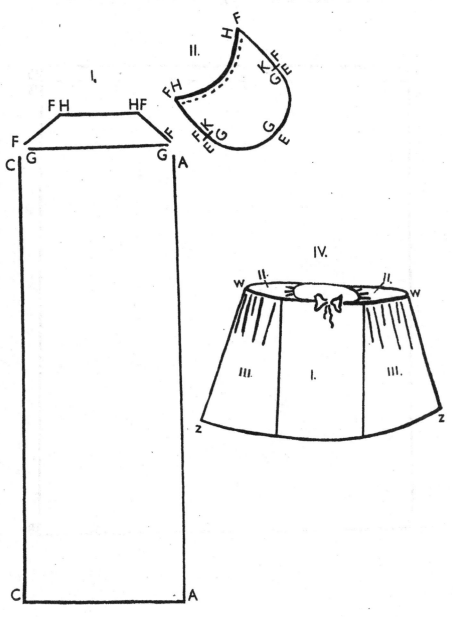

[*Diagrams continued overleaf.*

III.

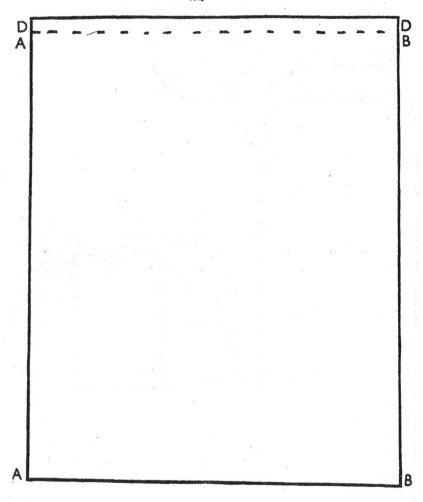

EIGHTEENTH-CENTURY LADY'S GOWN

(TO BE WORN OVER PANNIER PETTICOAT)
(For Diagrams see pages 134 and 135)'

SCALE—⅛ in. to an inch.
SIZE—Height, 5 ft. 6 in. ; chest, 36 in.
MATERIAL REQUIRED—*Gown*, 5¼ yds. material 48 in. wide.
Underskirt, 2½ yds. material 48 in. wide.
  I. Front of bodice. (Cut double.)
  II. Back of bodice.
  III. Sleeve.
  IV. Stomacher.
  V. Saddle.
  VI. Side panel of skirt.
  VII. Back panel of skirt.
METHOD—Join dart AAA in front of bodice. Join underarm seam BB and shoulder seam CC. Join sleeve seam DD. Insert sleeve in armhole. Face back bodice front EE and fasten with hooks and eyes. Interline stomacher with canvas and bone. Face back and attach to bodice point downwards. Place stomacher with centre top at top right hand front of bodice. Stitch down right side. Fasten left side with press-studs. Face back sleeve opening. The skirt is made from three widths of material 42 in. long. It is left open in front. Join three widths together. Double back side panel (Section VI.) at dotted line FF to make facing of front opening. Pleat skirt at dotted line GG on to saddle (Section V.). Make the point P in skirt (Section VI.) correspond with point P on centre circumference of saddle. Attach skirt to bodice pleating in fullness but sewing in saddle unpleated. The centre saddle H should correspond to seam of dart AAA in bodice front. Hem bottom of skirt. Finish bodice with ruffle of lace or muslin 4 in. deep at sleeve. Wear with fichu. Trim stomacher with small ribbon bows and jewels.
Underskirt—This is made from two widths of material 42 in. long. Join widths, hem bottom, face in top, and run draw-string through. If required, underskirt may be trimmed in front with loops of ribbon and bows to correspond with stomacher.

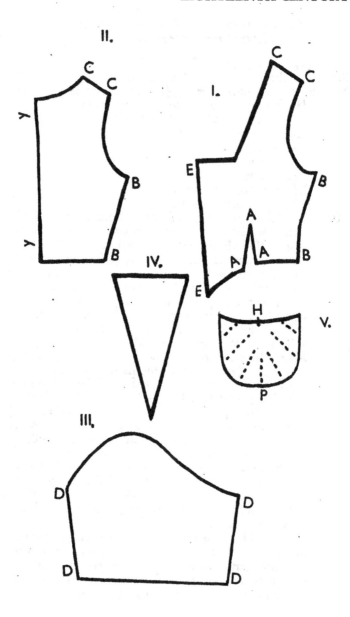

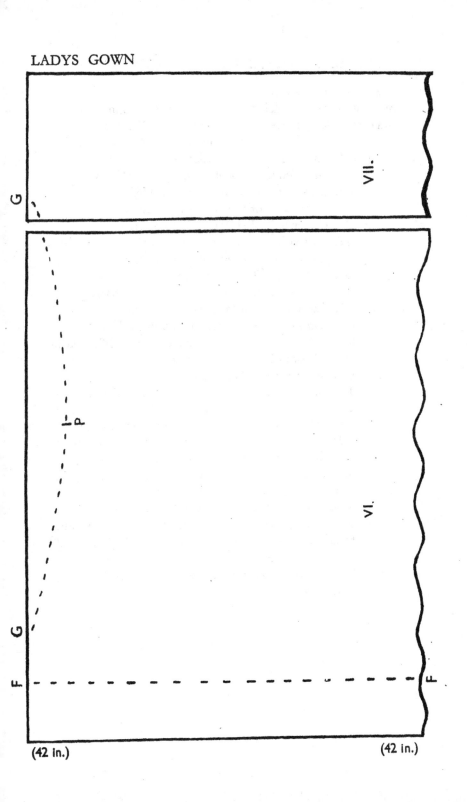

LADYS GOWN

NINETEENTH-CENTURY CUTAWAY COAT

SCALE—⅛ in. to an inch.

SIZE OF PATTERN—Height, 5 ft. 8 in. ; chest, 36 in. to 38 in.

MATERIAL REQUIRED—3 yds. of material 48 in. wide.

        3 yds. lining material 48 in. wide.

    I. Front of coat. (Cut double.)

    II. Under-arm panel of coat. (Cut double.)

    III. Back panel of coat. (Cut double.)

    IV. Upper half of sleeve. (Cut double.)

    V. Under half of sleeve. (Cut double.)

    VI. Half collar. (Cut in four pieces.)

METHOD—Join darts AAA and BBB in coat fronts. Tack down pleat CCCC, making fold lie towards centre back. Join under-arm panel (II.) to back panel (III.) at DDD. Join under-arm seam EE. Join shoulder seam FF. Repeat with other half coat, then join the two halves at centre back seam GG. Face HH. Make pleat JJ with outer fold towards centre in line with seam GG. Repeat on other coat tail. Join outside sleeve seam KK and inside sleeve seam LL. Insert sleeve in armhole. Join centre back seam of collar MM. Repeat with second pair of collar pieces. This makes outside and inside parts of collar. Interline one side with canvas. Join inside and outside together at NN, NN. Join collar to neck of coat. Double collar in half along dotted line. Face back fronts OO and double back revere along dotted line PP. Line coat throughout. Finish with two brass buttons on back pleats and two buttons each side front with corresponding buttonholes. The coat may be worn open or buttoned up.

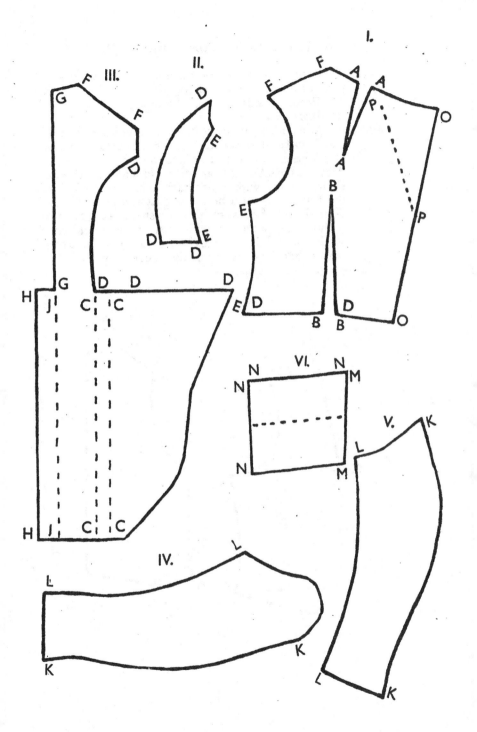

NINETEENTH-CENTURY WAISTCOAT

MATERIAL REQUIRED—¾ yd. of material 48 in. wide and
¾ yd. of lining material 48 in. wide.

    I. Front of waistcoat. (Cut double.)

    II. Back of waistcoat.

METHOD—Join under-arm seams AA and shoulder seams BB.
Face back fronts of waistcoat and bottom with remains
of material. Bind or face hem and back of neck.
Attach adjustable strap at point P in under-arm seam.
Fasten fronts with four buttons and buttonholes,
the top button and hole being at the point C. If
desired, the fronts of this waistcoat can be cut
without the points, in which case they should end
at the dotted line. This waistcoat may be worn
with either the Cutaway or the Frock Coat.

CODE—*y*, Fold of material.

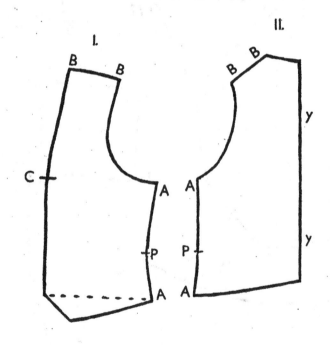

NINETEENTH-CENTURY MAN'S
DICKY SHIRT FRONT

SCALE—⅛ in. to an inch.
SIZE—Height, 5 ft. 8 in. ; chest, 36 in. to 38 in.
MATERIAL REQUIRED—⅛ yd. white cotton shirting.
⅛ yd. organdie 36 in. wide.
    I. Dicky front. (Cut double.)   II. Frill.
METHOD—Join two sides of dicky front all round. Make
studhole at A for fastening to neck-band of shirt.
Make buttonhole at B for fastening to bottom shirt
button. Double organdie down to centre. Join
all raw edges. Gather at CC. Draw up and attach
to dicky along dotted line DD. Sew ¼ in. band of
shirting over join to make neat finish. Sew four
pearl shirt buttons down this centre band at regular
intervals. Starch dicky stiffly. Goffer frill.
CODE—y, Fold of material

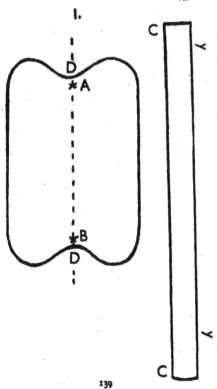

NINETEENTH-CENTURY TROUSERS

SCALE—⅛ in. to an inch.

SIZE OF PATTERN—Height, 5 ft. 8 in. ; chest, 36 in. to 38 in.

MATERIAL REQUIRED—3 yds. material 48 in. wide.

> ½ yd. black or brown elastic 1 in. wide.
>
> ¼ yd. lining material.

I. Front panel of leg. (Cut double.)

II. Back panel of leg. (Cut double.)

III. Buttonhole strip of fly front. (Cut single.)

IV. Button strip of fly front. (Cut single.)

METHOD—Join front and back panels at side seam AA and at BB to form one trouser leg. Repeat with other leg. Join two legs together at back seam from waist to crutch CC. Join fronts from bottom of fly to crutch DD. Face back fly-openings with lining material to fit Sections III. and IV. Face both fly strips. Cut and stitch buttonholes in Section III. Stitch into left side of fly-opening, insetting the strip so that the outer edge corresponds with edge of fly. Stitch corresponding number of buttons to Section IV., attaching the edge of the strip EE to the outside edge of right side of fly-opening. Tack down left edge of fly to edge of strip between buttonholes to prevent gaping. Face in waist and foot of trousers. Sew on braces buttons. Sew strip of elastic to pass under the foot to bottom of outer and inner leg seams so as to keep trouser down over instep.

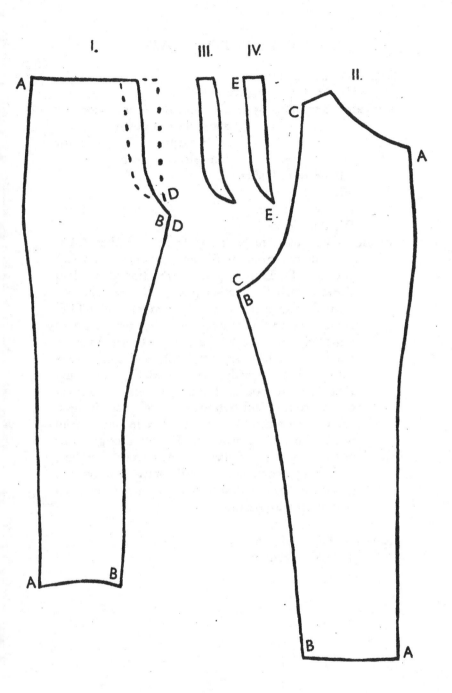

LADY'S EMPIRE GOWN

SCALE—⅛ in. to an inch.

SIZE—Height, 5 ft. 6 in. ; chest, 36 in.

MATERIAL REQUIRED—5 yds. material 36 in. wide for short-sleeved gown.

5½ yds. material 36 in. wide for long-sleeved gown.

I. Front of bodice.

II. Back of bodice.

III. Long sleeve.

IV. Puff sleeve.

METHOD—Join darts in back and front of bodice AAA. Join under-arm seam BB and shoulder seam CC. Join dart DDD in long sleeve (Section III.). Join sleeve seam EE. Gather puff sleeve (Section IV.) along dotted lines. Join under-arm seam of puff FF. Attach puff to top of long sleeve. Insert both into armhole. Face back opening in centre back of bodice GG and fasten with hooks and eyes. Make skirt from three widths of material 44 in. long. Pleat on to bodice leaving 6 in. placket at centre back. Hem bottom of skirt. Face in neck and run draw-thread through. Face in cuffs. Trim waist with fold of material. For evening gown or gown for young girl, cut neck to lower dotted line, omit long sleeve, and use puff only. For evening gown trim hem and neck with ruching of material caught up with pearls.

CODE—q, Top of sleeve.

y, Fold of material.

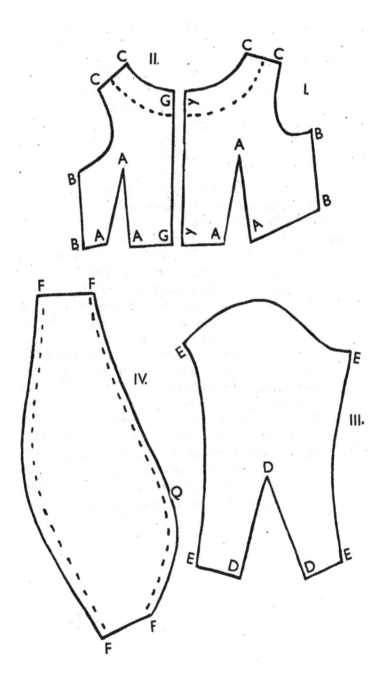

SCALE—⅛ in. to an inch.

SIZE—Height, 5 ft. 8 in. ; chest, 36 in. to 38 in.

MATERIAL REQUIRED—3 yds. material 48 in. wide.

3 yds. lining 48 in. wide.

    I. Front. (Cut double.)

    II. Side panel. (Cut double.)

    III. Back panel. (Cut double.)

    IV. Front skirt. (Cut double.)

    V. Under half sleeve. (Cut double.)

    VI. Upper half sleeve. (Cut double.)

    VII. Collar. (Cut double.)

METHOD—Join dart AAA. Join side panel (Section II.) to back panel (Section III.) at BB. Join under-arm seam CC and shoulder seam DD. Join front skirt (Section IV.) to back panel (Section III.) at EE. Make pleat along dotted line FF with fold in line with seam BB. Join front skirt to Section II. and I. at GG. Repeat with other half coat. Join centre seam HH, inner sleeve seam JJ, and outer sleeve seam KK. Insert sleeve in armhole. Face back cuff and front openings. Interline collar with French canvas. Join two halves at centre seam LL. Face lining on to collar. Sew collar into neck MM. Press back revere at dotted line NN. Fold back centre back skirt opening along dotted line PP, level with seam HH. Tack down top of fold under seam. Make buttonholes on left side at points OOO. Stitch buttons to correspond to right side.

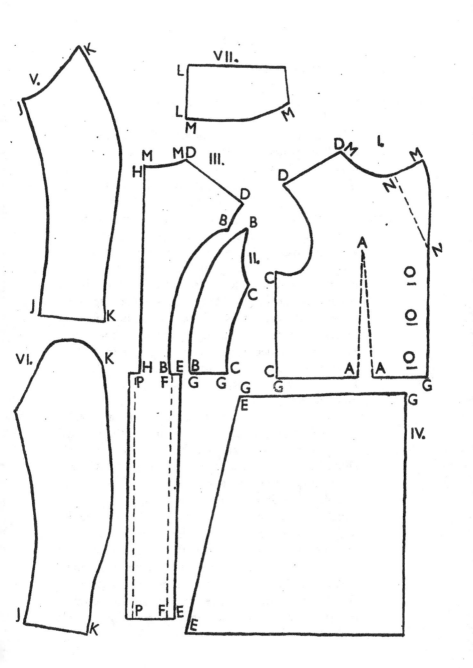

CRINOLINE

SCALE—⅛ in. to an inch.

SIZE OF PATTERN—Height, 5 ft. 6 in. ; chest, 36 in.

MATERIAL REQUIRED—5¼ yds. of material 48 in. wide.
    I. Front of bodice. (Cut double.)
    II. Under-arm panel of bodice. (Cut double.)
    III. Back panel of bodice. (Cut double.)
    IV*a*. Sleeve. (Cut double.)
    IV*b*. Diagram to show shaping of under-arm of sleeve. *This is not a pattern to be cut.*

METHOD—Join darts AAA, BBB, CCC. Join under-arm panel (II.) to back panel (III.) at DD. Join under-arm seam EE. Join shoulder seam FF. Repeat with other half of bodice. Join two halves of bodice at centre back GG. Join sleeve seam HH. Insert sleeve in armhole. Face back neck-opening, fronts and waist tabs of bodice with remaining pieces of material. Fasten fronts with hooks and eyes. Finish neck and sleeve edges with narrow pleated fold of material, stitched to inside edges, or bodice may be worn with lace collar and lace inner sleeves.

Skirt.—This requires no pattern as it consists merely of three widths of material 44 in. in length, gathered into a petersham waist band. One of the seams should be left open 6 in. for a placket, which may be worn either at the back or left side. The hooped crinoline petticoat should be made from three panels of sheeting 48 in. wide, each panel 44 in. long to correspond with the skirt. Hoops of crinoline wire should be run through tapes stitched to the inside of the petticoat at hip-level, knee-level, and at the hem. The circumference of the hoops should be adjusted to taste, but care should be taken not to make the hoop at hip-level too large, as this makes an ugly line.

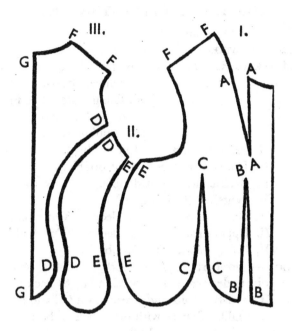

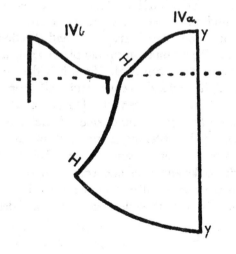

THE BUSTLE DRESS—THE BODICE

SCALE—⅛ in. to an inch.

SIZE OF PATTERN—Height, 5 ft. 6 in. ; chest, 36 in.

MATERIAL REQUIRED—5 yds. material 48 in. wide for complete dress.

   ¾ yd. lining material 36 in. wide for back panel of skirt.

   1 yd. crinoline wire.

 I. Front of bodice. (Cut double.)

 II. Under-arm panel. (Cut double.)

 III. Back panel. (Cut double.)

 IV. Fantail. (Cut double.)

 V. Under-arm section of sleeve. (Cut double.)

 VI. Upper-arm section of sleeve. (Cut double.)

 VII. Collar band. (Cut double.)

METHOD—Join dart AAA in bodice front (Section I.). Join under-arm panel (Section II.) to back (Section III.) at BB. Join under-arm seam CC and shoulder seam DD. Repeat with other half of bodice. Join two halves at centre back seam EE as far as dotted line. Join inner-arm seam FF and outer-arm seam GG. Insert sleeve in armhole. Join two halves of collar band HHHH. Attach collar band to neck of bodice. Face back fronts, cuffs, and bodice lapels. Join two halves of fantail (Section IV.) at LLL. Pleat fantail in sunray pleats graduating from ½ in. pleats at top MM. Face half the pleats from the right towards centre and half from the left towards centre of fantail. Do not pleat from the point P to edge on either side. Attach fantail under back lapels, stitching centre top of fantail under bottom of centre seam. Fasten fronts of bodice with hooks and eyes and trim with small buttons. A narrow lace collar may be turned down over collar band, with cuffs to correspond, if desired.

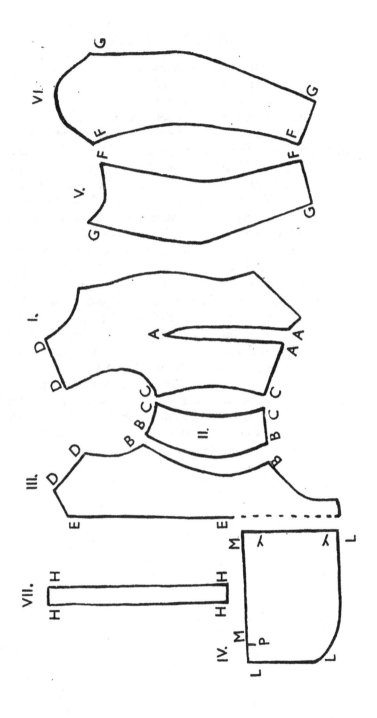

THE BUSTLE SKIRT

I. Front panel. (Cut double.)

II. Side panel. (Cut double.)

III*a*. Back panel. (Cut single.)

III*b*. Lining for back panel. (Cut single.)

Note.—This is a five-piece skirt with the seam centre front.

METHOD—Join front panel (Section I.) to side panel
(Section II.) at AA. Repeat with other front and
side panels. Join these to first pair at front centre
seam BB (*N.B.*—leave open 6 in. of left side seam
for placket). Tack tapes for wire inside lining
panel (Section III*b*) at dotted lines CC. Make flat
pleats in back panel (Section III*a*) at points PP with
folds lying towards hem. Stitch down folds, but
press only along edge of side seam. Out of spare
material make flounce frill and gather into back
panel at DDD. Join back panel (Section III*a*) to
lining (Section III*b*) at EE. Join front panels to
back panel and lining also at EE. Pleat front panel
(Section I.) and side panel (Section II.) at point PP,
and mount on petersham waist-band, making
fastening at left side seam. Face back hem. Run
wire through tapes in lining (Section III*b*). Attach
strings of tape at ends of wire, draw up slightly to
make bulge of bustle, and tie.

CODE—*x*, Hem of garment.

y, Fold of material.

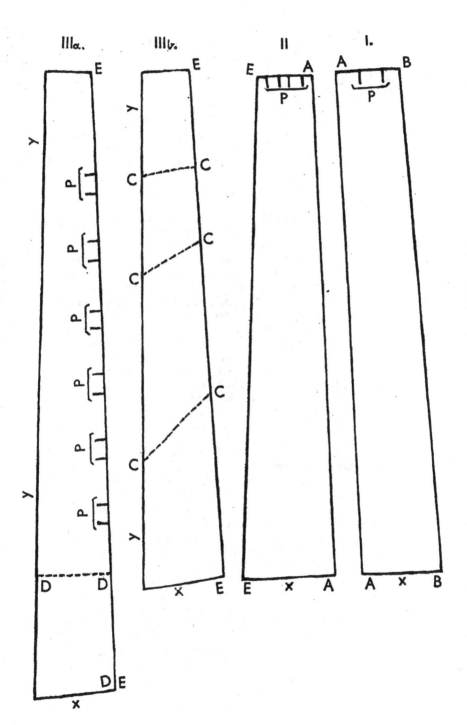

HOOD, CHAPERONE, TUDOR AND ELIZABETHAN CAPS

SCALE—⅛ in. to an inch.

MATERIAL REQUIRED—

    I. Hood.—¾ yd. of material 48 in. wide.

    II., III., and IV.—Chaperone, head-band, and liripipe.—1 yd. of material 48 in. wide. ¾ yd. of material 48 in. wide for facings.

    V. and VI.—Head-band and circular brim and crown for Tudor and Elizabethan flat caps. —½ yd. of material 48 in. wide.

METHOD—

    I. *Hood.*—Join back seam AA. Face back front opening and join with hooks and eyes or press-fasteners in front CC. Face back or bind hem.

    II., III., and IV. *Chaperone.*—Cut Section II. together with facings, either scalloping edge or leaving plain. Sew in facing along edges. Join side seam AA in facing and in upper part : run gathering thread round head opening BB. Pad head-band (Section III.), join ends CC. Tack in gathered head opening of Section II., BB. Double over and join DD. Join up seam EE of liripipe (Section IV.). Join end FF. Attach end of liripipe to join head-band, Section III., at CC.

    V. Head-band to Elizabethan cap.

    VI. Elizabethan and Tudor cap crowns.

Note.—The Tudor cap is shaped like a large tam o' shanter, with a brim of the same circumference as the top of the cap. The Elizabethan cap is shaped like a tam o' shanter without the brim, but with a head-band attached to the opening in the crown to secure a firm fit. In both these patterns the opening for the head must be adjusted to fit individual requirements.

    Tudor Cap (A).—The flat brim for the Tudor cap. It should be cut double and interlined with buckram. Seam up outer and inner edges.

        (B).—Crown of cap. Attach outer circumference of B to outer circumference of C.

        (C).—Lower side of crown : cut single and seam round outer and inner circumference of A.

    Elizabethan Cap.—Cut B and C and join round outer circumference. Cut head-band (Section V.). Join ends GG. Notch inner circumference (Section C), and tack to edge of head-band HH. Double head-band and stitch edges together.

CODE—y, Fold of material.

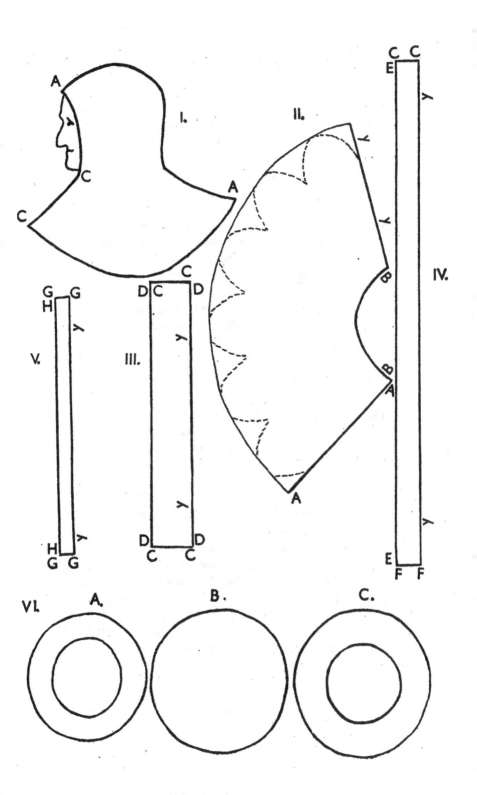

GABLE HEAD-DRESS AND FRENCH HOOD

i. *French Hood.*

    SCALE—⅛ in. to an inch.

    MATERIAL REQUIRED—1 yd. of velveteen 36 in. wide.
        ¼ yd. of contrasting material. Canvas.

      I. Halo.

      II. Forehead band.

      III. Hood.

      IV. Diagram showing completed head-dress.

    METHOD—Cut canvas interlining for halo, and wire edge
    with hat wire. Cover with contrasting material.
    Attach forehead band to halo AA. Seam hood of
    velveteen at BBB. Cut triangle CCC and bind edges.
    Sew hood to back of halo AA, the points DD being
    attached to either end of halo DD, and centre of hood
    opening E corresponding with centre of halo. The
    forehead band may be made either from velveteen or
    contrasting material.

ii. *Gable Head-dress.*

    SCALE—⅛ in. to an inch.

    MATERIAL REQUIRED—¾ yd. of material 48 in. wide, or
      1½ yds. of material 36 in. wide. Similar amount
    of lining material of a contrasting shade.

      V. Half-section gable front.

      VI. Head-band.

      VII. Hood.

      VIII. Diagram showing completed head-dress.

    METHOD—Cut canvas interlining for gable front (Section
    V.). Edge outside edge with hat wire. Cover with
    lining material. Cut semicircle of lining material
    AAAA. Tack into hood. Face tabs BBBB with
    outside material. Attach head-band (Section VI.)
    to gable (Section V.) at CCC. Attach head-band to
    hood (Section VII.) at DD. Double tab BBBB at
    dotted line, and attach at point P.

CODE—*y*, Fold of material.

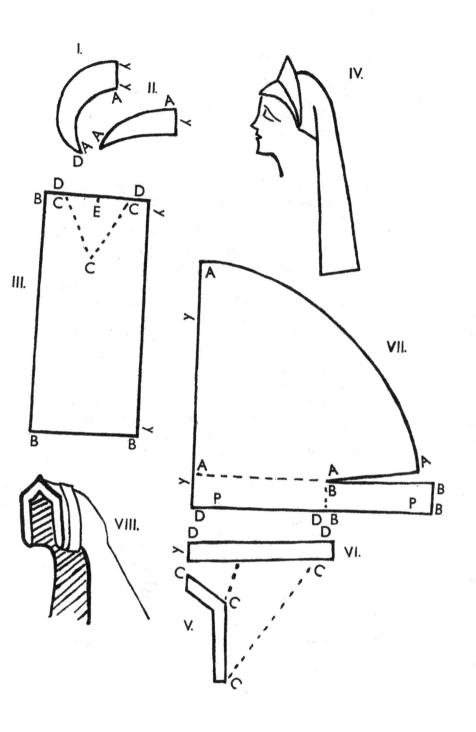

I.

II.

A

A

A

D

III.

B D D

C E C

C

B B

IV.

VII.

A

Y

A A A

Y B B

P B P B

D D B

D D

Y VI.

C C

C

V.

C

VIII.

THE HEART-SHAPED HENNIN

SCALE—$\frac{1}{8}$ in. to an inch.

MATERIAL REQUIRED—$\frac{1}{2}$ yd. material 36 in. wide; $\frac{1}{2}$ yd.
French canvas; $\frac{1}{4}$ yd. velveteen 36 in. wide.

    I. Heart shape.

    II. Roll.

    III. Diagram showing completed head-dress.

METHOD—Pad the canvas from within the rough circle
formed by the top of pattern and the dotted line AA.
Face with material so that padding is between canvas
and facing. Join the end and side-seam of roll, making a long tube; stuff this with wadding. Close open
end. Sew roll along top of heart-shape (Section II.)
at BB. Fasten head-dress at CC with hooks and
eyes, which should be adjusted to secure a firm fit
round the head. The heart-shape should be faced
with a patterned material in order to obtain a
contrast with the plain roll. This head-dress may
be worn with a veil as shown in the diagram, if
desired. For the veil a strip of chiffon or georgette
is required, $\frac{1}{2}$ yd. wide and 1 yd. long. Attach one
end of veil to inside lower edge of heart-shape,
allowing free end to drape over head and hang
down back. The veil should be of a pale shade.

CODE—y, Fold of material.

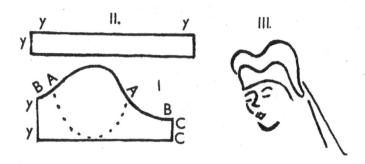

ELIZABETHAN WINGED CAP

SCALE—$\frac{1}{8}$ in. to an inch.

MATERIAL REQUIRED—$\frac{1}{2}$ yd. gold or silver or white lace 36 in. wide. Hat wire.

    I. Crown.

    II. Wing. (Cut double.)

    III. Diagram of completed head-dress.

METHOD—Make a circular frame of wire to fit the head, bending centre front into " widow's peak " with pliers. Bind edge of crown (Section I.) to wire frame all round. Make wire frame for wings. Bind each wing (Section II.) to wing frame. Attach wings to crown, attaching the point A to the widow's peak in crown. In order to get the wings to fit easily to the crown frame, it may be found necessary to ease the point A slightly with pliers.

CODE—y, Fold of material.

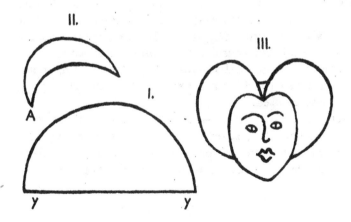

LIST OF MATERIALS SUITABLE FOR
EACH PERIOD

SAXON.—Woollen material of a rough plain weave, linen, plain silk for head rail. Materials should be un-patterned and in pure colours.

NORMAN.—Similar to above. The use of silk may be extended to the robes of the women.

HENRY II.–EDWARD I.—Figured materials of simple design may be added. Fur may be used for trimming.

EDWARD II.—Smooth weaved woollen materials such as face cloth and felt may be added. Parti-colouring permissible.

RICHARD II.–HENRY VII.—Patterned damasks. Heavy silks. Velvet and cloth of gold and silver permissible. Fine lawn or organdie for head veils.

HENRY VIII.–JAMES I.—Gold and silver braid. Jewels for ornamentation.

CHARLES I.–ANNE.—Materials chiefly without marked design. Self-patterned damasks, antique satin, velvet, woollen cloth. Organdie. For women, silk such as Poult de Soie, cushion silk, dull-surfaced satin.

GEORGE I.–GEORGE III.—Brocades, velvet, satin, moiré, woollen cloth. For women, taffeta and chintz may also be used.

GEORGE IV.–VICTORIA.—*Men*: Woollen cloth in plain weave. Rep, alpaca. *Women*: Cotton prints, light woollen materials printed in small designs. Satin, taffeta, lace. Checked silks were also popular.

A SHORT LIST OF BOOKS

TECHNICAL HANDBOOKS

ASHDOWN, MRS. CHARLES
BRITISH COSTUME DURING NINETEEN CENTURIES
T. Nelson & Sons Ltd.

BOEHN, MAX VON, AND OSKAR FISHEL
MANNERS AND MODES IN THE NINETEENTH CENTURY.
Four Volumes
J. M. Dent & Sons Ltd.

CUTTS, E. L.
SCENES AND CHARACTERS OF THE MIDDLE AGES
D. O'Connor
(Out of Print)

FAIRHOLT, F. W.
COSTUME IN ENGLAND. Vol. I. History
G. Bell & Son Ltd.
Vol. II. Glossary
(Out of Print)

KELLY, F. M., AND R. SCHWABE
HISTORIC COSTUME, 1490-1790
B. T. Batsford Ltd.

KÖHLER, CARL
A HISTORY OF COSTUME
G. G. Harrap & Co. Ltd.

QUENNELL, C. H. B. AND M.
HISTORY OF EVERYDAY THINGS IN ENGLAND
B. T. Batsford Ltd.

GENERAL READING

PERIODICALS: PUNCH *and* THE ILLUSTRATED LONDON NEWS
THE PASTON LETTERS
DIARY OF SAMUEL PEPYS
DEFOE—JOURNAL OF THE PLAGUE
DEFOE—MOLL FLANDERS
DE COVERLEY PAPERS
RICHARDSON—CLARISSA HARLOWE
RICHARDSON—SIR CHARLES GRANDISON
FIELDING—TOM JONES
FIELDING—JOSEPH ANDREWS
GOLDSMITH—VICAR OF WAKEFIELD
LAURENCE STERNE—SENTIMENTAL JOURNEY
FANNY BURNEY—EVELINA
BOSWELL—LIFE OF SAMUEL JOHNSON
WORKS OF JANE AUSTEN
WORKS OF CHARLES DICKENS
MEREDITH—RICHARD FEVEREL